The Gardening Goddess Guide to Edible Gardening *in Portland*

JOLIE ANN DONOHUE

The Gardening Goddess Guide to Edible Gardening in Portland

Copyright © 2021 Jolie Ann Donohue

The Gardening Goddess is a trademark of Jolie Ann Donohue
and The Gardening Goddess Books

All rights reserved. No part of this book may be reproduced without written permission from the publisher, except by a reviewer who may quote brief passages with appropriate credits; nor may any part of this book be transmitted in any form or by any means, electronic or mechanical, including photocopy, recording, or any other information storage or retrieval system without written permission of the publisher.

The information in this book has been carefully researched and is true and complete to the best of our knowledge. All recommendations are made without guarantee on the part of the author or publisher. The publisher and author assume no responsibility for any injuries suffered or for damages or losses incurred during the use of or as a result of following this information. It is important to study all directions carefully before taking any action based on the information and advice presented in this book.

The Gardening Goddess Books
www.jolieanndonohue.com

Keywords for *The Gardening Goddess Guide to Edible Gardening in Portland*
1. Vegetable Gardening 2. Organic Gardening 3. Herb Gardening 4. Regional Gardening: Oregon

ISBN-13: 978-0-578-50505-3

Dedication

This book is dedicated with gratitude
to my sweetest love, Jay,
the best partner in love, life, and gardening.

Acknowledgments

I am fortunate to live and garden in Portland, Oregon on the unceded lands of the Multnomah, Kathlamet, Clackamas, Cowlitz Band of Chinook, Tualatin, Kalapuya, and Molalla peoples. With reverence, I acknowledge these cultures, these communities, elders both past and present, future generations, and their land. I acknowledge my living here as a guest is founded upon the exclusions and erasures of many Indigenous peoples, and we must begin the process of working to dismantle the ongoing legacies of settler colonialism.

This book is a true labor of love many years in the making. Thank you to my many gardening students, garden consultation and design clients, and readers for your loyalty, enthusiasm, and curiosity. Thank you for inspiring me to continue learning and growing.

Thank you to my best friend Catherine for encouraging me to never give up on my dreams and to strive to be my most authentic self in everything I do. Thank you to my "framily"—the best support system a person could ever have: Carrie, Krista, and Lori. Thank you, Jeanine, Erin, Adrienne, Katie, Jessica, Mary D. and my home group for keeping me solidly in one-day-at-a-time.

The skills and inspiration of my writing coach Becca Deysach helped me with my discernment that led to the first vision of this book. Thank you to the many friends who read and edited the initial publication proposal for this book, including my friend and colleague Peggy Acott. Thank you, Erika W., for supporting my many gardening and writing endeavors through the years. Thank you to my first editor and friend Crystal, who believed in me and my work, nurtured an incredible vision for this book, and enthusiastically collaborated towards making my dream a reality. I am indebted to my talented and efficient copy editor Cleo Hehn and book designer Ryan Forsythe.

Thank you to Alida and Jennifer at PDX Writers for awarding me the Cecilie Scott-Betsy Milligan scholarship, for helping me to find my voice, and for nurturing my writing in such a warm and inviting environment.

My husband Jay and I share a life rooted in the love of gardening and the natural world. I am eternally grateful to Jay, my strongest cheerleader, and the many sacrifices he has made so I could finally bring this book to the world. Thank you for believing in me every time I stopped believing in myself.

Thank you to the many gardens I have planted and tended the past twenty plus years. Gaia Mother Earth and her nature continue to be one of my greatest teachers. I am grateful for my sacred work as a steward of this beautiful planet.

—*Jolie Ann Donohue, The Gardening Goddess*

Contents

SECTION TWO

10 / A-Z Guide to the Best Vegetables for Portland   **133**

11 / A-Z Guide to the Best Herbs for Portland   **195**

Introduction

Welcome to *THE GARDENING GODDESS Guide to Edible Gardening in Portland!* I am happy you are here, happy we are sharing this exciting gardening journey together. Many years ago, my friends began calling me their personal gardening goddess. Every place I went, friends, acquaintances, neighbors, the grocery store cashier (you get the picture!) would ask me their gardening questions. In 2015, I started my own small business and named it The Gardening Goddess.

Growing up in the suburbs of the San Francisco Bay area, I did not experience gardening or know anyone that gardened, even though my mother grew up on a farm in Nebraska. When I was growing up in the 1970s, it was very much a part of middle-class culture to keep "moving up" from humble roots on a farm, so gardening was not a consideration. I had no idea what a farm was or where my food came from. The closest thing to "gardening" I ever witnessed was my father mowing our perfectly green chemically treated lawn. In my life there was no real connection to the earth.

I began gardening in my twenties when living in San Francisco. My flat had a small backyard with a wild postage-stamp garden. There was fragrant Mexican sage, sensual calla lily, prickly cactus, rambunctious pink climbing rose, and the entire back fence was covered in stunning flaming red zonal geranium climbing six feet tall.

Daily I sat on the deck smoking cigarettes and looking at what I then thought of as an overgrown mess, and after a few months, I decided to clean it up. My favorite secondhand bookstore supplied me with three gardening books. I cleared the center of the postage-stamp and planted seeds for lettuce, carrots, and radishes. Cleaning up this secret garden awoke and inspired the gardening bug deep buried deep in my spirit.

This started a whole new routine in my life. Public transportation and walking were my commute methods in San Francisco; hardly anyone I knew owned a car except my roommate. On Saturday mornings I would borrow her car early in the morning before she woke up, and I'd jam across to the other side of the city to visit a garden center. I purchased terra cotta pots, soil, and a variety of herbs and annual plants. Potting up and caring for these plant babies became a priority. I enjoyed spending hours in my tiny garden when no one else I knew was gardening or talking about gardening. I learned from reading gardening books and slowly nurtured my new passion. It even helped me to quit smoking!

When I moved to Portland in 2000, most of those container plants accompanied me in the moving truck on the journey northward. They lived with me on the stoop of my first three apartments, and the container collection continued to grow. When I moved into my first duplex in Outer Southeast, I acquired a large yard. I built two raised beds and cleared some grass for an in-ground herb garden. My container garden overflowed down the steps of the large front porch.

Around this time, I became increasingly frustrated with my career as a professional "helper." When the 2006 recession hit, I was laid off from two jobs in a row due to budget cuts. I took a seasonal job at a local nursery that I intended to be at for less than six months while I pursued a permanent job in human service. Here I am, thirteen years later, having unexpectedly made a midlife career change to horticulture. Nature works in mysterious and magical ways.

Working in nurseries and floral shops for seven years surrounded me with plants and flowers daily. I tended, discussed, and studied plants. Going back to school, I earned certificates in home horticulture, horticultural therapy, and modern organic farming on small acreage. I became known as the "veggie gardening go-to gal" at my nursery, as staff and customers both sought me out for expert advice. Even friends on social media in other parts of the country would reach out to me for advice and guidance.

Over the next couple of years, I built more raised beds, gardened in more containers, and was a founding member of two community gardens. Garden design and maintenance, in addition to my full-time nursery job and school, completely saturated me in horticulture. I loved it!

Ultimately, I started my own consulting business, providing therapeutic horticulture, garden design, floral design, edible garden consultation, and workshops around the Portland metro area. I married a gardener, and we continue to build as many gardens as we can in our small urban rental. I still get asked gardening questions most places I go. I live, breath, drink, and sleep gardening, and it is a wonderful life. Nature has the inherent power to heal our lives and our earth.

Most people assume I have a huge garden. My 136-square-foot edible garden consists of four raised beds, close to fifty containers of all sizes, and two small in-ground spaces nearby the raised beds. I raise at least fifty percent of our food and have plenty left over for preserving or giving to friends.

When I began gardening, it was not a popular hobby or trend for city-dwelling twenty-somethings like myself. I was self-taught through books and experimenting. In my thirties in Portland, I began to build my community of gardening enthusiasts. I frequently tell my gardening students and clients that gardening is an experiential skill, learned through doing, through trial and error. Everyone makes mistakes; it is an important part of the process. Even now that I'm The Gardening Goddess, I still kill plants and have gardens that fail to thrive. We can learn from both our successes and our failures. This learning is cumulative, and every year I have more skills and knowledge to keep my garden thriving. I don't believe in the concept of green or non-green thumbs. Don't give up, just keep gardening and having fun.

This book is the culmination of my twenty-five years of gardening experience and twelve years of teaching gardening workshops specific to the Portland metro area. I began dreaming up this book in 2015 when I took the leap of faith to leave my full-time job and start my own business. I am happy to share this gardening adventure with you.

Warmly,
Jolie Ann Donohue
The Gardening Goddess

Healing People, Communities, and the Earth One Garden at a Time

Section One

1 / The Goddess's Organic Gardening Basics

MOST DEFINITIONS OF ORGANIC GARDENING say that it is the lack of using synthetic fertilizer, pesticides, and herbicides in the garden that makes it organic. But organic gardening is so much more than what it is not. An organic edible garden aims to grow the safest, healthiest food while being environmentally friendly. An organic garden is both a balanced and biodiverse ecosystem. Biodiversity is defined as a variety of life in the world or in a particular habitat or ecosystem.

A naturally grown biodiverse edible garden incorporates an abundance of vegetables, fruit, herbs, and flowers. Organic gardening is about being a steward of our soil, beneficial bugs, birds, and other wildlife. An organic garden is productive, healthy, and beautiful.

Technically, a gardener can be "organic" and still introduce a tremendous amount of organically approved sprays into their garden. Over twenty years ago, I began as a traditional gardener and did not have a clue about organic gardening. When I decided to switch to organic gardening to be "healthier," I simply replaced my synthetic sprays with organic sprays. For years, I continued to bomb my garden with sprays as the solution to any pest or disease problem without considering the impact on my small garden ecosystem.

Some years ago, I was studying soil health and fertility in a course about modern organic farming on small acreage. Around the same time, I was deeply affected by the highly publicized plight of bees dying in massive numbers when spring flowering trees in a shopping center parking lot were sprayed with a synthetic and highly toxic pesticide.[1] A movement has grown to ban these neonicotinoids. I knew then I wanted to minimize my use of any sprays and promote a more natural garden. This was a huge philosophical shift, and in practical matters, it dramatically changed every way I implement gardening.

Transitioning from 'organic' to 'no-spray natural' in my garden has been a fun, challenging, and rewarding adventure. I hope my experience and the tips and techniques included in this book inspire you to plant a biodiverse edible garden grown organically with minimal to no use of sprays.

Putting the right plant in the right place

In my observations, most gardeners who don't succeed struggle because they didn't keep in mind the simple principle of "right plant, right place." Bearing in mind the particular needs of each edible plant, such as sunlight, soil, nutrients, watering, placement, and growing season, does not need to be complicated. I find the simpler I keep it in the garden, the happier and more successful I am. So, let's dig in together with some basics.

Edible plants need soil, nutrients, sunlight, water, and fresh air. Most all vegetable and herb plants need a full sun location. Your edible garden will receive the most sunlight and thrive in a southern exposure location.

By a full sun location I mean 8-10 hours of sun per day. Even if it rains or is cloudy, that is okay, as long as for 8-10 hours a day your garden is not shaded by a fence, house, tree, or other tall structure. Examples of some popular edible plants that require a full sun location to produce: tomatoes, corn, cucumbers, squash, eggplant, and peppers.

Some edible plants will do well in a full or partial sun location, meaning the garden receives 4-6 hours of sunlight per day. This could mean either shade in the morning with sun in the afternoon, or vice versa.

Tolerate partial sun:

- **Chard**
- **Collards**
- **Lettuce**
- **Kale**
- **Peas**
- **Radishes**
- **Salad greens**
- **Scarlet runner beans**
- **Spinach**
- **Most herbs**

Need full sun:

- **Tomatoes**
- **Corn**
- **Cucumbers**
- **Squash**
- **Eggplant**
- **Peppers**

---

1 Specter, Dina, 2013, June 20. 25,000 Bees Died In This Parking Lot Because Landscapers Allegedly Didn't Read Insecticide Instructions, *Business Insider*. https://www.businessinsider.com/death-of-thousands-of-bees-due-to-insecticide-2013-6

Examples of some popular edible plants that would do well in 4-6 hours per day of sunlight: chard, collards, lettuce, kale, peas, radishes, salad greens, spinach, 'scarlet runner' beans, and most herbs.

When considering a site to build your garden, you may not have a lot of choice. Ideally, you want to choose a site as close to your home as possible and near an accessible water source. The closer your garden is to your home, the more likely you are to care for it, and the closer the hose is to your garden, the more likely you are to consistently water.

I always advise new gardeners to start small. One to two garden beds the first year is practical and manageable, giving you an accurate sense of the amount of time and effort it takes to maintain your vegetable garden. Armed with this valuable experience, you can always expand later.

In my experience, gardeners are naturally ambitious. Can you relate? I have heard many of us pronounce during our first time gardening that we will grow all the food to feed our family on our own urban homestead. That's a wonderful dream, and while I don't mean to be discouraging, my wish is for you to be successful first. The more modest your initial garden, the greater your chance of being successful. Success builds on success. Before you know it, you will feel confident enough to tackle four raised beds, a small berry patch, and even a couple of dwarf fruit trees.

When building your garden, keep in mind pathways between garden beds should be wide enough to comfortably accommodate you and a wheelbarrow. That's a minimum of 2.5 feet. To keep down on weeds, place a barrier on paths such as landscape fabric, newspaper, or cardboard, and cover the barrier with bark mulch, bark nuggets, or gravel. I know this is not the fun stuff of planting vegetables; however, thoughtfully preparing paths when you build your garden will save you a lot of extra work later on.

Garden beds, either in-ground or raised, should be no wider than four feet. That ensures the garden is easily accessible and that you can reach in two feet from each side. Weeding, planting, or harvesting in beds wider than four feet require you to walk onto or crawl into the garden, and that causes soil compaction. Garden beds can be any length. Some garden beds are 4-by-4 feet, 4-by-6 feet, or 4-by-8 feet.

How to decide between raised beds and in-ground beds? I expand more on this in the Small Space Gardening chapter, but here's a brief comparison:

RAISED BEDS: Raised beds are an excellent solution for compacted soils and poor drainage. Gardening is higher and can be more ergonomic for the body than in-ground gardens. Raised beds keep gardens up out of the way of dogs. On the other hand, the initial investment is higher for raised beds versus in-ground gardens.

Read more about raised beds and in-ground gardens in Chapter 3.

IN-GROUND BEDS: The initial cost of an in-ground

garden is less expensive because you are not buying wood or filling raised beds with planting mix. On the other hand, building an in-ground garden can mean more tedious physical labor if the soil needs to be tilled and the site needs to be cleared of plants, weeds, or debris.

The dirt on healthy dirt

Healthy soil equals healthy plants. I cannot stress this enough. Healthy soil is the most critical ingredient for successful gardening. Did you know that one gram of healthy soil is home to as many as 500 million little creatures like worms, bacteria, fungi, yeast, protozoa, and algae? These soil organisms create and maintain the complex warehouse and distribution system of nutrients that feed your plants. That's a lot of good guys integral to the garden ecosystem, and as organic gardeners, we want to keep them happy.

In the Portland metro area, the native ground soil is primarily clay. The other end of the soil spectrum is sandy soil. In the middle is the ideal soil type: loam. Getting to an ideal soil balance takes dedication and time. Our clay soil holds a lot of water, does not well drain, and is easily compacted. As you can imagine, clay soil contributes to shallow root systems, inhibiting root growth and causing plants to rot during wet weather.

Improve clay soil by amending it with lots of organic matter like compost, aged manure, earthworm castings, coir, pumice, sand, and greensand. These sources of organic matter will assist in breaking apart clay and improving drainage, and all are available at gardening centers around the area. Planting deep-rooted cover crops will also assist in breaking up clay soil and improving drainage.

Portland area native soil also tends to be slightly acidic. This is great for acid-loving plants like blueberries, rhododendrons, azaleas, camellias, and gardenias. Not so much for vegetables: vegetables prefer a more neutral pH. You can "sweeten" your acidic garden soil by adding agricultural lime when you build your garden and annually at planting time. A box of agricultural lime has quantity instructions and is also available widely at gardening centers.

If you have inherited a filled raised bed, or if the bed is older and your plants aren't producing, you may want to pH-test your soil. It is also recommended to test pH when building a new in-ground edible garden. A simple pH test kit from your local nursery is inexpensive and should do the trick. Make sure to take multiple samples to test from each area of the garden.

Working in your garden when the soil is wet, as well as walking on garden beds in any weather, causes soil compaction. Wait until your soil is dry to till, dig, or plant. Portland is famous for our wet rainy springs, and if we were to wait for our soil to dry out on its own, that could mean waiting until June or July! In the early spring, you can help your garden dry out by covering the soil with a tarp or cardboard weighted down. I would recommend doing this in early March for planting cool season vegetables, and in early May for planting warm season vegetables.

To prepare your in-ground garden or build raised beds, you need to remove weeds and grass by tilling, hoeing, or pulling by hand. Remove rocks, trash, and debris. You will sometimes find an array of construction debris on a newly built lot.

Should you till or "turn" the garden bed to prepare for planting? Yes and no. Using a rototiller or shovel to turn soil can make the situation worse, and at the same time, it is also harmful to all those 500 million beneficial organisms. Gardens don't necessarily need or benefit from tilling. For the small space urban gardener, I advocate no-till methods.

If you have a brand-new or very neglected garden, I recommend initially tilling and incorporating compost to start your garden. After that, I advocate using no-till methods to improve your soil structure. I never recommend tilling in a raised bed, as it is difficult to

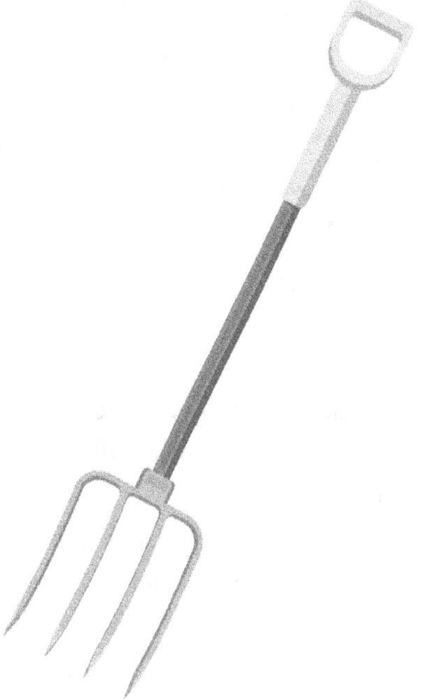

maneuver. Some no-till gardening methods include using a broadfork or spading fork, planting cover crops, amending with compost and organic matter, and sheet/lasagna mulching.

Using a spading fork or broadfork will gently loosen the soil and assist in amending it with compost or other organic matter. I love using my spading fork in raised beds and in-ground gardens. It is super easy to use and doesn't take a toll on my back. A broadfork is a larger tool used by farmers and is an excellent option for in-ground beds.

Adding 3-4 inches of compost initially and then 1-2 inches annually will promote healthy garden soil. You can add compost any time of year; however, the optimal time is when the soil has warmed up to at least 55 degrees, in mid to late spring.

Read more about fertilizer in Chapter 4.

Fertilizer is another consideration when preparing the garden soil. Fertilizer is not plant "food." Plants make their own food. Fertilizer provides nutrients to assist your plants in manufacturing what they need to be healthy so they can grow and grow. Different plants use different nutrients at different rates. More fertilizer is not better. Avoid over fertilizing by following package instructions.

Remember to use **organic** fertilizer. An organic fertilizer is made from plant, animal, or earth ingredients like alfalfa meal, blood meal, or rock phosphate. A synthetic or conventional fertilizer is composed of human-created chemicals.

A fertilizer package will contain three numbers, for example: 5-10-5. These three numbers refer to N-P-K levels.

- **N**=Nitrogen. Promotes leaf growth. Sources: alfalfa meal, bat guano, blood meal, feather meal
- **P**=Phosphorus. Promotes root and bloom. Sources: bone meal, fish bone meal, rock phosphate, seabird guano
- **K**=Potassium. Promotes overall plant health. Sources: glacial rock dust, greensand, kelp meal

In addition to N-P-K, there is a multitude of trace minerals that plants need in smaller quantities to thrive. Excellent sources of these micronutrients are in kelp meal (dry) or liquid seaweed. I especially like to use liquid seaweed to water new transplants to promote their root growth.

Fertilizer is either water-soluble or water-insoluble. Liquid seaweed, fish emulsion, liquid bat guano, and compost tea are all water-soluble. These liquid fertilizers make nutrients immediately available to your plants. Fertilizer can also come in granular, water-insoluble forms, like alfalfa meal, bone meal, blood meal, and kelp meal. These granular fertilizers slowly release their nutrients to your garden plants. Granular fertilizer mixes contain multiple nutrients and come pre-packaged in boxes or bags. Several companies produce organic vegetable garden fertilizers. There are even vegan fertilizer formulas that do not contain animal ingredients.

Fertilizer will include instructions with application rates. As a general rule, I apply organic granular fertilizer every 4-6 weeks during the active growing season. If you are using organic liquid fertilizer, apply every other week during the active growing season for most vegetables.

For simplicity, purchase the pre-packaged organic vegetable garden fertilizer at your local garden center. This keeps it simple and sets you up for success. If you are interested in experimenting, many local nurseries carry bulk individual fertilizers. I mix my own custom granular fertilizer with alfalfa meal, rock phosphate, greensand, kelp meal, and lime. For liquids I like using liquid seaweed, an organic liquid fertilizer for bloom and fruit growth, and compost tea. You do not need to use all of these fertilizers to be successful. I find it fascinating to study about soil life and fertility. I really like to get to know my soil.

Beginner's gardening tool kit shopping list:

- ❑ Trowel (hand-held shovel)
- ❑ Cultivator (hand-held tool)
- ❑ Round head shovel (I look for the lighter weight smaller blade size)
- ❑ Spading fork
- ❑ Stirrup oscillating hoe
- ❑ Bow rake (has short rigid metal tines)
- ❑ Watering wand and garden hose
- ❑ Pruners

Notes

Notes

Notes

2 / Small Space Urban Gardening

SEVERAL YEARS AGO, I DESIGNED a curriculum and started teaching a gardening class about how to successfully garden in small spaces. This class was prompted out of my experience as an avid gardener. Twenty-five years of gardening in the full spectrum of living situations can teach a person a lot. This includes container gardening on the front stoop of my apartments, participating in two urban community gardens, farming every inch of an uncultivated backyard at a rental house, and creating my current garden. For eight years, I have lovingly tended a bountiful garden and joyfully lived in our secret garden cottage.

Four mature maple trees mostly shade our yard. We squeeze out veggies and herbs from every available spot of sunshine. Over the years of working as a gardening teacher, more and more students of my veggie gardening 101 class kept asking about how to garden in containers, how to garden indoors, and how to garden in one raised bed. All of these experiences culminated in my popular small space gardening class.

If you think you don't have room to garden, I challenge you to reexamine your space. In our current yard, the only sunny garden space is along the pathway on the south side of the house. When we moved in, this area had two neglected raised beds and a brick pad used as storage for a composter and numerous trash and recycling bins. This was the hottest, brightest spot in the yard, and it was not being utilized to its fullest gardening potential.

In small spaces, the gardener is challenged to really prioritize their needs and wants. It takes a good amount of organization and planning to not end up with a jumbled, overcrowded mess of plants competing with each other. Every year I tweak and replant this evolving garden to meet our needs. It takes some creative thinking to re-imagine the existing space into potential new gardening space as our needs grow and change.

I had dreams of an ornamental flower garden to nourish bees, butterflies, and hummingbirds as well as provide me with cut flowers for my design work. I envisioned a bed overflowing with my favorite flowers: sunflowers, dahlias, lilies, poppies, and peonies. So we removed a very old, rangy, four-foot tall and wide rosemary shrub that consumed all the space, extended the gardening bed a few feet into unused space, and lined the area with a river rock border. Viola! I had a new 4-by-6 foot flowerbed.

In a very sunny spot of the side yard stands a huge red flowering rhododendron. It is pretty for its few weeks of bloom in May, but after that, its evergreen leaves take up prime sunny space. Rather than remove it, I drastically pruned it from the bottom and within to open up its shape. This has scored me an additional 3.5-by-5 feet of gardening space. Due to the rhododendron's mature root system, I strategically planted annual flowers, instead of perennials, and maximized the sunny space by lining it with small containers.

Moving the composter to an unused part of the yard opened up space to build my third raised bed for vegetables that can tolerate bright indirect light and partial shade. Moving the trash and recycling bins to a new part of the yard opened up a very warm sunny space for my potato tubs and a fourth raised bed.

In another area of the yard were three stunted, unproductive old blueberry plants, overgrown roses that never bloomed, ferns, ground cover, and weeds. This area only receives bright indirect sunlight. Last year, I removed the old blueberry plants and cleaned out everything else. After adding new compost and a brick lined border, the result was a 3-by-3 foot patch in which I originally experimented with strawberries, but there was not enough sunlight. This became the perfect spot for my seven pots of mint and lemon balm. Right next door to this project is a 3-by-5 foot bed of mature raspberries that produce like crazy twice a year in the part sun/shade location.

> **Even the smallest garden can yield the satisfaction of growing some of your own food.**

By planting two new blueberry bushes in large pots, I was able to move the pots around annually until finding the perfect location for both space and sunlight.

All four raised beds have a trellis along the backside for vines like peas, beans, and flowers. Utilizing vertical gardening maximizes limited space. Three of the four raised beds are reserved for vegetables with companion plant herbs and annual flowers. One raised bed is reserved for my perennial herbs with annual herbs added each spring.

The raised beds total 92 square feet of growing space. An additional 20 square feet is reserved for containers and 24 square feet of ground space for berries. This provides a total of 136 square feet of growing space for edibles.

In this little amount of space—only 136 square feet—I am able to grow the following:

Vegetables

Arugula	Kale	Potatoes
Beans (pole and runner)	Leeks	Radishes
Beets	Lettuce	Rutabaga
Broccoli	Mache	Shallots
Carrots	Mesclun Mix	Spinach
Celeriac	Onions	Summer Squash
Collards	Orach	Swiss Chard
Cucumbers	Parsnips	Tomatoes
Garlic	Peas	

Fruit

Blueberries	Raspberries	Strawberries

Herbs

Basil	Lavender	Parsley
Chamomile	Lemon balm	Rosemary
Chervil	Lemon verbena	Sage
Chives	Lovage	Savory
Cilantro	Marjoram	Scented geraniums
Dill	Mint	Tarragon
Fennel	Oregano	Thyme

That's a lot of variety and quantity of fresh, delicious food!

As I've demonstrated, growing vegetables does not require large amounts of space. Even the smallest garden can yield the satisfaction of growing some of your own food. This is great news for urban gardeners growing food in smaller spaces like containers, raised beds, community gardens, and small in-ground gardens. The challenges of small space gardening can be overcome with planning and creativity. Focusing on planning and preparing, we will learn to grow amazing and productive small space food gardens that are robust and resilient in their biodiversity.

Container gardens

Container gardens can be grown where traditional gardens are not possible, including apartment balconies, small courtyards, decks, patios, and areas with poor soil. Containers are an ideal solution for people with rental situations, with limited mobility, or with limited time to care for a large landscape. Perhaps the only sunny spot in your yard is your driveway. This is another opportunity to try a container garden.

There are many types of containers that are suitable for edible gardens: plastic pots, terra cotta pots, glazed ceramic pots, pulp pots, wood barrels, planter boxes, wire baskets lined with sphagnum moss or coconut coir, galvanized metal troughs, or even cement blocks. All-natural fabric containers are durable and lightweight, a perfect container for growing edibles. And unlike plastic, they are naturally BPA free.

Since you are growing edibles, make sure to never use a container that held toxic materials such as chemicals, paint, cleaning products, herbicides, pesticides, fungicides, petroleum products, or medication. It is not a good idea to grow edibles inside of old tires.

Container considerations

No matter what container you select, it is important to consider drainage. Plants will not grow successfully in soil that is continually water-logged. If there is no existing drainage hole in the container, make multiple holes in the bottom.

Consider whether your pots will be moved during the growing season. When water is added to soil in an already heavy container, the weight may be too much to easily lift. Keep in mind that tall plants require a heavier container to avoid tipping over from imbalance. Containers of minimum size hold less moisture, especially when the roots are crowded. Small containers will need more daily maintenance during the heat of summer. Consider using a slightly larger container with more soil to hold moisture and reduce maintenance.

As an organic gardener, you will need to decide whether you think plastic containers are safe for growing your edibles. You may be concerned about plastic leaching into the potting soil and into your food. I think this is a valid concern. Many gardeners use five-gallon buckets, some will avoid them. Never grow food in a plastic container if it was used to hold pesticide, herbicide, motor oil, paint, etc. I do not claim to be an expert on gardening safety in plastic containers or on their potential toxicity. Please do your research and use your own best judgment. If you are concerned about growing edibles in plastic, then don't do it.

Plastic pots that say PET are made of polyethylene terephthalate. You can identify PET by locating a triangle and the number 1 on the bottom of your container. PET is used in soft drink, water, and beverage bottles as well as peanut butter and other food containers.

Plastic pots that say HDPE are made of high-density polyethylene. You can identify HDPE by locating a triangle and the number 2 on the bottom of your container. HDPE is used in milk jugs, juice and water containers, and most five-gallon food buckets. At a local nursery, I have found propagation and decorative pots made from HDPE.

Plastic pots that say LDPE are made of low-density polyethylene. You can identify LDPE by locating a triangle and the number 4 on the bottom of your container. LDPE is used in bread, frozen food, and grocery bags.

Plastic pots that say PP are made of polypropylene. You can identify PP by locating a triangle and the number 5 on the bottom of your container. PP is used in caps, lids, deli soup, syrup, yogurt, and margarine containers. At a local nursery, I have found potato grow bags, living wall systems, and 20-gallon black plastic tree pots made of PP.

Terra cotta pots are made of clay that is fired but not glazed. Cheery rusty orange and natural looking, they are the classic garden pot. Terra cotta pots always remind me of red geraniums, and they were the very first container I began gardening with back in 1995. Terra cotta has moderate weight and is relatively inexpensive. However, since terra cotta is not glazed, the clay absorbs water and can freeze in cold winters, expanding and breaking the pots. Depending on the size of the terra cotta pot and the sun location, it may need more frequent watering than other types of containers.

Glazed ceramic is beautiful and available in a wide range of colors and styles. These containers can help a patio garden look more sophisticated. Glazed ceramic is more expensive than other options, and large pots are very heavy once filled with soil and plants. But they are more tolerant of cold weather and need less frequent watering than terra cotta.

Pulp pots are made from molded recycled waste paper and are biodegradable. An Oregon-based company, Western, manufactures their pulp pots in the USA. I have purchased them from local nurseries. Pulp pots are inexpensive and are very lightweight. They are not good for long term gardening as they eventually biodegrade. I also do not recommend pulp pots for patio gardens, as they will make a big mess once they begin biodegrading.

I have gardened extensively with pulp pots and found them to last about two years before breaking down. They are a nice option for someone who wants to experiment with edible container gardening without making a large initial investment.

Wooden planter boxes and half wine or whiskey barrels are a natural-looking addition to the container garden. You can find affordable half wine or whiskey barrels at local nurseries. Since they were used to ferment grapes into wine, the wood may still contain fungus. Before filling these planters with soil, consider first wiping them down with vinegar. Wooden planter boxes come in squares and rectangles in a variety of sizes. Look for planter boxes made from naturally rot-resistant cedar or redwood. Never grow edibles in wood that has been treated or painted as toxic chemicals can leach into the soil and into your food. You can use a non-toxic eco-friendly wood stain on planter boxes.

Wire hanging baskets lined with moss or coco liner are a beautiful and fun way to incorporate vertical gardening into your small space garden. I like growing strawberries, herbs, salad greens, and edible flowers in wire baskets. There are even container varieties of cucumbers and tomatoes that would be successful in a wire basket. Poking several holes around the sides of the moss or coco liner makes more room for plants and adds interesting visual appeal. Wire baskets can be reused from year to year by inserting new moss or coco liner.

Galvanized metal troughs for edible gardening are all the rage in the Portland area. You can find galvanized metal containers at local nurseries and agricultural supply stores. They are relatively lightweight and affordable, no assembly required. This can be good news if building raised beds seems daunting. They come in a variety of shapes and sizes and are at an ergonomic height for raised gardening. Like with other containers, drill holes for drainage.

Some gardeners have expressed concern about zinc leaching into the soil from galvanized containers. Galvanization is the process of coating steel with zinc to resist oxidation and prevent corrosion or rusting. Livestock eat and drink out of these galvanized troughs. Galvanized steel is used for nails, metal-framed buildings, air ducts, cables, coiling, and streetlights. Most garden tomato cages are made from galvanized metal. If you are gardening in a used galvanized container, always know its history and confirm that it was not used to hold toxic chemicals. If you are concerned about zinc leaching in galvanized containers, don't garden in them.

What's in your potting soil? Hint: It's not soil.

Commercial potting soils are typically a combination of ingredients that hold water well like peat moss, coco coir, or ground bark, as well as ingredients that prevent compaction like perlite, vermiculite, or pumice. Additionally, potting soil may contain earthworm castings, compost, sand and/or a fertilizer. I like to choose organic potting soil for my edibles. In this case, the term "organic" is referring to the fertilizer contained in the potting soil.

When it comes to filling up your containers for edible gardening, use a good quality organic potting soil. This may be packaged as potting soil, potting mix, or soilless planting mix. Do not worry too much about terminology. Container gardens require potting soil that is specially formulating for container gardening. Even though the bag says "soil," potting soil does not actually contain any soil. What? Now, *that* is confusing!

Do not use native ground soil or top soil in containers as it has a high percentage of clay particles that easily compact, reducing oxygen that is available to the roots. Additionally, native soil may contain disease, microorganisms, insects, and weed seeds unfit for container gardening. Packaged topsoil is too dense for container gardening. Packaged and bulk "compost" four-way/three-way planting mix is intended for amending your raised beds or in-ground garden, not for container gardening. I recommend disposing of the used potting soil in your edible gardening containers every one to two years and starting new with fresh potting soil. To prevent waste, I add the used potting soil into my home compost maker or spread around the top of my ornamental in-ground garden.

Vegetables well-suited to containers:

Beets	Kale	Radishes
Carrots - especially	Lettuce	Salad Greens
smaller varieties	Mustard Greens	Scallions
Collards	Peppers	Spinach
Eggplant	Potatoes	Swiss Chard
Fennel	Radicchio	Turnip

The following vegetables can successfully grow in containers, as long as you follow these suggestions:

- Peas and beans can be grown in a larger container fitted with a tripod for the vines to grow up.
- Look for container varieties of cucumber, tomato, and zucchini.
- I have grown tomatoes in large 10-gallon plastic pots fitted with a tomato cage. In my experience, cherry tomatoes do best in containers.
- Most herbs are well suited to growing in containers.

These edible plants just don't do well in containers:

- Asparagus is a perennial crop that needs an exclusive, deeply dug, well-prepared, in-ground or raised bed to thrive
- All melons grow on large and sprawling vines. In the last year, however, I've seen container varieties available.

- Pumpkins and winter squash grow on large and sprawling vines. Again, in the last year, I've seen container varieties available.
- Corn plants are too tall for most containers, and you need to closely grow several plants for good wind pollination.
- Cabbage and cauliflower plants are too big for most containers, and each will only yield one head per plant.
- Artichokes are really tall and wide perennial plants, and most containers would not be large enough. You could try them in a sturdy wine barrel, but keep in mind, they are a tender perennial and are more prone to freezing in containers than in-ground.

Raised bed gardens

Raised beds have many benefits for gardeners, especially in small space gardens. They are a great solution for compacted soils or if soil contamination is questionable. Their taller size makes gardening more ergonomic for aging backs and knees. Once filled with a compost mix, raised beds are ready for immediate planting. Raised bed soil warms up quicker in the spring and means earlier planting, and it is easy to keep optimal conditions in a raised bed.

Raised beds need to be built to a minimum of 18 inches tall to grow most vegetables. The recommended height is 2 to 4 feet tall. Naturally rot-resistant cedar and redwood are great long-lasting woods, though they are more expensive than most other woods. Douglas fir is the next best option for raised bed lumber. Pine is inexpensive but will decompose quicker than cedar, redwood, and doug fir. In my opinion, cedar, redwood, and doug fir are great investments for homeowners, and pine is an affordable option for renters. Avoid using pressure-treated wood or railroad ties as they can leach arsenic into the soil. Do not paint your raised beds for the same reason. Raised beds can be coated with a non-toxic eco-friendly stain.

Raised beds should be no more than 4 feet wide, so that you can reach in 2 feet from each side. Raised beds can be any length you choose. 4-by-6 feet and 4-by-8 feet are pretty standard sizes. If beds are only accessible from one side, they should only be 2 feet wide.

Prepare the area where you intend to build raised beds. To remove sod and weeds, you can use a rototiller or hand tools. You can also use cardboard boxes or newspapers as a grass and weed-smothering barrier at the bottom of raised beds. I recommend this extra measure of protection after removing weeds and grass. Do not use herbicides to kill grass and weeds in an area you are going to grow food.

Raised beds do not require potting soil. They should be filled with planting mix or compost blend formulated for raised beds. If you want to fill your raised beds with native soil from your yard, add two parts compost to one part native soil. You can purchase packaged raised bed planting mix from a local nursery. A more affordable option is purchasing bulk planting mix from a local soil company.

Careful consideration of size at maturity and growth habit will help you determine which edible crops to include in your container and raised bed gardens. Some edible crops stay petite at harvestable maturity like radishes, lettuce, and basil. Other edible crops are space hogs like long vining winter squash and pumpkin.

In a small space garden, I am always thinking creatively about how to best use the space I have for a more abundant harvest. One technique I use is companion planting, planting two or more kinds of plants together in one area based on the way individual crops grow and their size at maturity. For example, I might combine beans growing up on a trellis, with alternating rows of lettuce and carrots underneath. This companion planting technique utilizes the garden space with plants that climb up, grow roots underground, and grow greens above ground. More information can be found about companion planting in Chapter 3.

Another technique I utilize in small spaces is vertical gardening. You can invest in or build a vertical growing system. Think creatively about how to incorporate simple trellises, tripods, and hanging baskets for plants that like to climb or hang. Some great edible plants for a hanging basket are lettuce, salad greens, mesclun mix, strawberries, nasturtium, container varieties of cucumber or cherry tomato, and basil.

My best tip for keeping my raised beds performing at their peak is taking care of my soil. As we learned in the first chapter, healthy soil equals healthy plants. I use organic and no-till gardening methods for optimal soil health. I garden in spring, summer, and fall seasons. During the winter I let my raised beds and containers rest with the exception of the perennial herbs and overwintering veggies, like garlic and shallots. Every spring, I add a fresh load of organic compost to top dress the raised beds. I incorporate organic fertilizer, compost tea, crop rotation, companion planting with lots of annual flowers, cover crops in the fall, and sheet mulching. We will learn more about all of these techniques in Chapter 7.

Getting the most from your small space garden

For several years, I had great fun volunteering with a non-profit urban agriculture program where I collaborated with a diverse group of new gardeners from over twenty countries, helping them plan, grow, and harvest in a community garden to feed their families. The edible plants that would yield the most food in a small space were super important to the success of these urban gardeners. Together, this is what we discovered.

In a small garden, these plants will yield the MOST food:

Beans - pole & bush	Kale	Summer squash &
Beets	Lettuce	zucchini
Carrots	Potatoes	Swiss chard
Collard & mustard	Peas	Tomatoes
greens	Rutabagas & turnips	
Herbs	Radishes	

These plants will yield a MODERATE amount of food:

Asian greens	Garlic	Shallots
Broccoli	Kohlrabi	Strawberries
Celery	Leeks	
Cucumber	Onions	
Eggplant	Parsnips	
Fennel	Peppers	

These plants take up a lot of space and yield LITTLE food in a small garden:

Artichoke	Melons and	Rhubarb
Corn	watermelon	Winter squash
Cauliflower	Pumpkins	

Notes

Notes

Notes

3 / Garden Planning and Design

NOW THAT WE'VE LEARNED about what makes up a biodiverse garden, vegetable growing basics, preparing the garden, and small space considerations, let's take it to the next step with the fun stuff: plants! In this chapter we will get an introduction to individual crops, growing season and planting times, crop rotation, companion planting, and succession planting. Together we will explore how you can design a planting plan for the most bountiful harvest and healthy garden.

A good place to start when dreaming up your garden plan is to browse seed catalogs and visit plant nurseries to get an idea about what you would like to grow in your garden. Think about what tastes best when it is directly from the garden, like sugar snap peas, tomatoes, cucumbers, and fresh herbs. Consider what crops you like to eat and what you would like to experiment with growing.

We gardeners are passionate people—we can get overzealous about the exciting prospect of growing so many types of vegetables. I'll say it again: Set yourself up for success by starting small. You can always expand your garden later. It's tempting to buy 10 tomato plants from the nursery when the staggering and exciting abundance of colorful tasty varieties is so enticing, but **one healthy tomato plant can yield 20 to 30 pounds of tomatoes in a season.** I know I am guilty of this in my own garden and have learned through hard knocks that 2 to 3 tomato plants is more than enough to feed my small family, to preserve, and to share with friends.

By learning about the individual growth habits, size at maturity, and days to maturity, you can begin to narrow your garden dream list. As we dig deeper into edible gardening, you will become familiar with which crops grow as vines, large bushes, low growing greens, underground roots and tubers, etc.

Edible crops run the full spectrum of plant size at maturity from the tiny underground radish to the rambling pumpkin vine. Days to harvestable maturity vary widely, from one month for quick growing arugula to four months for long season parsnip.

Root crops like beets and carrots prefer to be directly seeded in the garden. Summer crops that require a long hot growing season like tomatoes, peppers, and eggplant need to be planted in the garden as seedlings/transplants. Beans and peas are easy to start by direct seeding in the garden. Lettuce, kale, and other greens are successful both by direct seeding and planting transplants.

Hardiness zone, growing season, and frost dates

Here in Portland we are lucky to garden in the mild weather of USDA hardiness zone 8. My NE neighborhood sits in zone 8b and this means my annual extreme minimum temperature is 15 to 20 degrees F.

When we talk about the growing season, we typically mean beginning at the average last frost date and ending at the average first frost date. In Portland this means our growing season is approximately March to October. When I first began gardening in Portland, printed and online sources cited our average last frost date as April 15 and average first frost date as October 15. To confuse matters, in printed literature and online you will now see a wide range of average first frost dates for Portland from October 15 to December 15.

In my experience based on the last few years, our average last frost date falls around March 15 and our average first frost date falls around November 15. Therefore, our growing season for optimal temperatures is about March 15 through November 15.

Let's define frost temperatures and why it is even important. 36 degrees is a light frost, 32 degrees is frost, and 24 degrees is a hard freeze. Most edible plants will not grow in frost temperatures, and some will outright die. In frosty temperatures, soil is slow to warm up and seed germination is stunted. For optimal crop success, knowing your frost dates is important.

However, we should also take into consideration day lengths. Our peak sun exposure and longest day length falls annually on the summer solstice around June 20. From the spring equinox, annually around March 20, until the autumn equinox, annually around September 20, our gardens will receive the most sunlight.

Portland average high/low temperatures and days of rainfall		
January	46/37° F	14 days
February	51/39° F	12 days
March	56/41° F	14 days
April	61/44° F	12 days
May	67/49° F	9 days
June	73/53° F	5 days
July	80/57° F	2 days
August	80/58° F	2 days
September	75/54° F	5 days
October	63/48° F	9 days
November	52/41° F	15 days
December	46/37° F	15 days

Average annual rainfall = 35.98 inches
Average annual snowfall = 4 inches

A microclimate is a smaller area within a general climate zone that has its own unique climate zone. Microclimates can have differences in temperature, frost dates, and weather. Many factors influence microclimates, including elevation, topography, the presence of building materials like asphalt and concrete, and proximity to bodies of water. For example, within the city of Portland, microclimates exist within the Pearl District, the West Hills, inner Southeast, and outer Northeast. Similarly, there are differing microclimates between Corbett, Oregon City, Vancouver, Wilsonville, and Hillsboro.

An annual plant is one with a life cycle of one season or one year and then it dies. A perennial plant is one that will come back year after year.

While our growing season extends from March to November, please keep in mind not all edible plants will grow and thrive at any time during the season. Some crops prefer the cooler weather of spring and fall, while some crops require the hot temperatures of summer, and another class of crops are fall-planted so that they can overwinter for harvest the following spring or summer. Learning which crops grow best in each season will set you up for success.

An annual plant is one with a life cycle of one season or one year, after which the plant dies. A perennial plant is one that will come back year after year. Perennial plants can be herbaceous, meaning they die to the ground in the winter, or evergreen, meaning they retain stems and leaves all year long. Most vegetable crops are annual plants.

Cool season crops planted in early spring (March/April/May)

Arugula	Endive/escarole	Potatoes*
Asian greens	Florence fennel	Radicchio
Beets	Kale	Radishes
Broccoli	Kohlrabi	Salad greens
Brussels sprouts	Leeks	Scallions
Cabbage	Lettuce	Spinach
Carrots	Mesclun mix	Swiss chard
Cauliflower	Mustard greens	Turnip
Cilantro	Parsnips	
Collards	Peas	

** Plant potatoes in the spring for a summer harvest.*

Hot season crops planted in late spring (May and June)

Basil	Eggplant	Sweet potatoes
Beans	Gourds	Tomatoes
Cantaloupe	Ground cherries	Tomatillos
Celery	Peppers	Watermelon
Corn	Pumpkins	Winter squash
Cucumbers	Summer squash	Zucchini

Cool season crops to plant in June and July for a fall/winter harvest

Broccoli	Cabbage	Potatoes**
Brussels sprouts	Celeriac	Rutabaga
Cauliflower	Parsnips	

*** Plant potatoes in the summer for a fall harvest.*

Cool season crops to plant in August and September for a fall/winter harvest

Arugula	Kale	Radicchio
Asian greens	Kohlrabi	Salad greens
Beets	Lettuce	Scallions
Carrots	Mesclun mix	Spinach
Collards	Mustard greens	Swiss chard
Endive/escarole	Peas	Turnips
Florence fennel	Radishes	

Plant in September and October to harvest next spring

Fava Beans	Leeks	Shallots
Garlic	Onions	

Overwintering varieties of broccoli, cauliflower, cabbage, carrots

Perennial crops—plant in early spring (March/April/May)

Artichokes	Rhubarb	Sunchokes
Asparagus	Sorrel	
Cardoon	Strawberries	

Plant growth habits and heights

Tall crops: Brussels sprouts, corn, tomatillos, tomatoes

Tall vining crops: Peas, pole beans

Medium height: Broccoli, bush beans, cabbage, cauliflower, celery, collards, eggplant, fennel, garlic, kale, leeks, mustard greens, onions, peppers, potatoes, shallots, summer squash, Swiss chard, zucchini

Short height: Beets, carrots, celeriac, kohlrabi, lettuce, parsnip, radish, rutabaga, salad greens, scallions, spinach, turnip,

Wide sprawling vines: Cucumber, melon, pumpkin, winter squash

---

A good garden plan, even in the smallest of gardens, will incorporate biodiversity by utilizing companion planting. Companion planting is a technique based on a long history of observations of the interaction between plants in the garden. Certain combinations of plants can promote the abundance and health of edibles in your garden by altering the soil, attracting or repelling insects, and creating a helpful microclimate.

Companion planting

For centuries, gardeners all over the world have used companion planting. Some plant relationships have been scientifically proven, while others have been developed by trial and error over hundreds of years. Sometimes people refer to this information as old wives' tales. Older women are the wisest people I know, so I think that term is the highest compliment. Remember, just because it is folklore doesn't mean it does not work!

Some benefits of companion planting are fragrance, efficient use of resources, providing physical support and space, increasing biodiversity, and attracting/maintaining beneficial bug populations.

Plants that have strong fragrance like marigolds, chives, and thyme can confuse or detract pest insects from the crop they are looking for. Allium family plants like chives and garlic are reported to keep aphids off your roses. Brightly colored yellow and orange marigolds with their stinky strong aroma have long been planted in the vegetable garden to keep away pests.

Grouping together vegetables that have similar needs for fertilization, water, sun, and soil pH means an efficient use of resources. Cucumbers, lettuce, and celery require consistent heavy watering. Placing them together as companion plants makes it easier to water effectively.

Planting crops for culinary recipes makes for a fun themed garden. Companion planting tomatoes, garlic, and basil make it easy to harvest for pizza or marinara sauce. Likewise, a garden or container companion planted with baby lettuce, arugula, radishes, and edible flowers make a simple harvesting salad garden.

Companion planting herbs and flowers with your vegetables increase biodiversity in your garden. Planting a wide variety of plants in your garden is more consistent with how plant environments would naturally grow. Monocrop culture invites pests and disease. Continually planting the same plant year after year in the same place results in reliance on chemical herbicides, pesticides, and fungicides. With a biodiverse garden, you will attract more beneficial bugs, and pests will have a harder time locating the crop they are seeking.

> **The Gardening Goddess's companion planting method is interplanting vegetables with annual flowers and herbs to promote a healthy and vibrant garden.**

Putting the good bugs to work

We want beneficial bugs in our garden, and companion planting is one technique to attract and maintain beneficial populations of pollinators, predators, and composters.

Pollinators play an absolutely vital role in the garden. Without pollinators there would be no flowers and no fruit. One in three bites of food we eat is courtesy of pollinators. Some favorite vegetable garden crops like zucchini, cucumber, and pumpkins have separate male and female flowers on the same plant. A pollinator is required for these plants to produce fruit. A few garden pollinators are bees, wasps, butterflies, flies, and beetles. Hummingbirds and bats are also pollinators. Bees are the primary pollinator for most wildflowers and agricultural crops in the United States. In addition to the well-known European honeybee, there are four thousand types of bees native to the U.S.[2]

Predatory beneficial bugs help control pest populations in our garden by eating bugs we don't want. Ladybugs, lacewings, praying mantises, dragonflies, and spiders are all garden predators. Ladybugs, also called lady beetles, are actually beetles, and not all are females as their common name implies. They are the most well-known garden predator. Both larvae and adult ladybugs are hardworking garden predators with voracious appetite for aphids, eating as many as 5,000 aphids during their one to three year lifespan. Ladybugs will also eat other bugs that we don't want, such as mealybugs, leafhoppers, and mites.

Garden composters like worms help to break down organic matter and provide the garden with nutritious compost. Worm castings, sometimes known as vermicast or vermicompost, are a rich and potent organic source of nutrients for our plants. As worms eat through organic matter in the soil, the digested waste product is loaded with refined minerals and trace elements in their most usable form. Thank you, worms!

A diverse gathering of bugs promotes a healthy organic garden buzzing and humming with life. I've developed a deep reverence for the beneficial bugs that promote a balanced ecosystem in my garden.

To attract and keep beneficial bugs in your garden, consider their needs for food, water, and shelter. You will never attract ladybugs to your garden if you do not first tolerate some of their favorite food—the dreaded aphid! If you spray organic or conventional pesticides on your garden, you are killing off the food source for beneficial bugs, as well as disrupting the natural balance of the garden.

---

2 Native Bee Biology, Xerces Society for Invertebrate Conservation, https://xerces.org/pollinator-conservation/native-bees/

You can provide beneficial bugs with water sources at two levels. Place glazed saucers directly on the soil in raised beds and in-ground gardens. Add small pebbles and rocks to the saucers to make water accessible to bugs of all sizes. Keep these saucers frequently filled when you do your garden watering. Adding some sand to the saucers provides a source of trace minerals for thirsty butterflies. Raised bird baths around the garden assist flying bugs. The birds in my garden enjoy these so much, I refresh them daily with the garden hose.

Avoiding fall cleanup of your ornamental garden and leaving leaf and plant debris can provide winter shelter for some beneficial bugs. Planning a garden that is inviting to beneficial bugs means planning plants and environments for all their life stages. Including host plants in your garden ensures a home for eggs and larvae for a variety of beneficial bugs. I plant dill for ladybugs and grow milkweed and *centranthus* for butterflies. Be prepared for heavy munching on your host plants by larvae. Butterflies also need nectar plants for the adult phase of their lives.

Plant to increase biodiversity in your garden. In my edible garden, I mix vegetable crops with annual flowers and herbs. I plant a perennial flower bed close by. When we plant in a monocrop method, our edible gardens are more susceptible to pests and disease. By planting a biodiverse garden of vegetables, fruit, herbs, perennials, and annual flowers, we are mimicking Mother Nature's design. Aim for flowers with a succession of bloom from spring, summer, and fall. A biodiverse garden is more appealing to a wide variety of beneficial bugs.

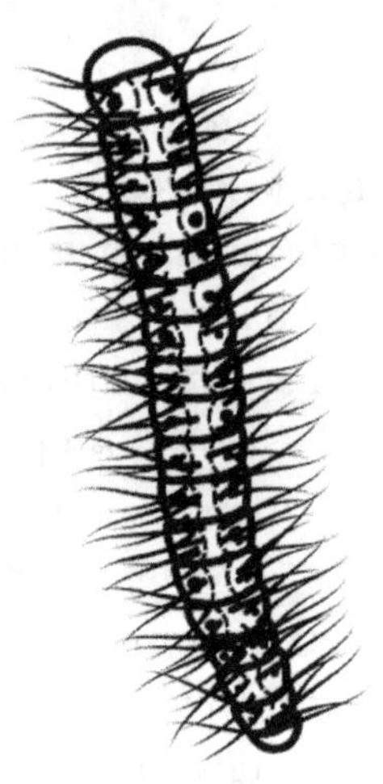

Some beneficial bugs, like butterflies, have other specific needs. Butterflies like warm sunny spots sheltered from the wind to do their basking. When temperatures are cooler, butterflies need to warm up their flight muscles and blood by basking their wings open to soak up warmth from the sun. To help with this, place large stones on the ground throughout your garden, ideally south facing. The stones will heat up in the sun and provide a perfect place for butterflies to bask in the warmth. This also provides a great viewing opportunity for you.

Some of my favorite plants for attracting beneficial bugs to my vegetable garden:

Annuals: alyssum, bachelor buttons, calendula, cleome, cosmos, lantana, petunia, nasturtium, sunflower, verbena, and zinnia

Herbs: basil, catnip, chamomile, dill, lavender, lemon balm, parsley, mint, oregano, rosemary, thyme. Note that mint and lemon balm aggressively spread by underground runners and are best contained by growing in a pot.

Perennials: *Asclepias, Aster, Achillea, Agastache, Coreopsis, Echinacea, Gaillardia, Leucanthemum, Monarda, Nepeta, Rudbeckia, Scabiosa, and Sedum.*

Letting these vegetable and herb plants go to flower and seed will attract beneficial bugs: arugula, broccoli, cilantro, lettuce, and mustard greens.

Flowering cover crops: Austrian peas, crimson clover, Dutch white clover, fava beans, mustard, lacy phacelia.

> **I never recommend borage or bronze fennel because they rapidly self-seed and become a menace in the garden.**

Crop rotation

Crop rotation is the practice of alternating crops to different garden beds from year to year. The crop rotation method I use is rotating entire plant families. This gives soil a rest from each vegetable family before that family appears in the same garden space again. Other gardeners rotate based on the root/shoot/fruit; in this method plant families are combined. There are many benefits of crop rotation, including reducing pests and disease and improving crop yields. Crop rotation works for annual vegetable crops, not perennial plants.

Many pests are attracted to a specific family of plants, such as aphids to *Brassicaceae* and leafminers to *Chenopodaceae*. By annually rotating crops, pests have a harder time finding suitable host plants and therefore cannot build up their numbers as quickly.

Most fungal disease stays in the soil and targets specific plant families, such as powdery mildew to the *cucurbitaceae* family. When we water the garden, fungus can be splashed from soil to plant leaf to plant leaf. By annually rotating crops, the fungal disease is deprived of its host plant and might not continue to build up in the soil.

Each plant family uses different nutrients at different rates from the soil. Some plant families are known as heavy feeders, such as *Solanaceae*. When annual crop rotation of plant families is utilized, yields are improved because nutrients in the soil are used more evenly.

> *Read more about fertilizer in Chapter 1.*

Vegetable Fertilizer Needs

Heavy feeders: Asparagus, broccoli, Brussels sprouts, cauliflower, celeriac, celery, corn, cucumber, eggplant, melon, pepper, pumpkin, tomato, tomatillo

Medium feeders: Beet, cabbage, garlic, kale, leeks, mustard greens, onions, Swiss chard, summer squash, winter squash

Low feeders: Basil, beans, carrot, Florence fennel, herbs, radish, kohlrabi, lettuce, parsnip, peas, potato, rutabaga, salad greens, spinach, turnip

Boost nitrogen in soil: Peas, beans, and cover crops: Austrian pea, crimson clover, Dutch white clover, fava bean

Ideally, crop rotation is on a 4-year cycle, meaning a plant family does not return to a garden area for four years. This works really well if you have 4 in-ground or raised beds. Even a 2-year rotation is better than none at all. This is most practical if you are gardening in, say, two raised beds.

It is possible to practice some crop rotation even in the smallest garden. If you are gardening in containers, replace the potting soil every year. With fresh soil, you do not need to rotate crops. Even removing up to half the soil and replacing with fresh planting mix and compost will help.

If you grow so much of one family that a 4-year rotation is impossible, try to put plants in a new place within the same garden bed every year, or take a 1-year break from growing an entire plant family. If you grow mixed plantings throughout your garden, consider noting things that you like to plant next to each other, and start moving those groups together as you rotate.

With a little thought and planning, crop rotation does not have to be complicated. Keep in mind, some plant families are more important to rotate than others, and follow these simple tips:

1. Get to know what crops are in each plant family.
2. Pick your companion planting herbs and flowers.
3. Group together your edible crops and companion plants.
4. Rotate this entire group each year.
5. Swap out individual crops within the same plant family.

Plant families

Alliaceae: "the allium family"
   Asparagus, chives, garlic, leeks, onion, scallion, shallot

Apiaceae: Carrot, celery, celeriac, cilantro, dill, fennel, parsley, parsnip

Asteraceae: Artichoke, chicory, endive, escarole, sunchoke, lettuce, radicchio

Brassicaceae: "the *Brassica*, cabbage, crucifer family"
   Arugula, broccoli, Brussels sprouts, cabbage, cauliflower,
   choi, collards, cress, kale, kohlrabi, mizuna, mustard, oilseed
   radish (cover crop), radish, rutabaga, turnip

> **Brassicaceae is the most important family to rotate.**

Chenopodiaceae: Beet, chard, spinach

Convolvulaceae: Sweet potato

Cucurbitaceae: "the cucurbit or squash family"
   Cucumber, gourd, melon, pumpkin, summer squash,
   winter squash, zucchini

> **Cucurbitaceae is the second most important family to rotate.**

Fabaceae: "the bean or legume family"
   This family actually benefits the soil and doesn't need rotating.
   Beans - all types of pole, bush, drying, fava, runner
   Peas - all types of sugar snap, snow, and shelling
   Cover crops - Austrian peas, crimson clover, fava beans, Dutch white clover

Poaceae (formerly *Gramineae*): Corn, cover crops such as annual ryegrass, fall cereal rye

Solanaceae: "the nightshade or solanum family"
   Eggplant, ground cherry, potato, pepper, tomatillo, tomato

> **Solanaceae is the third most important family to rotate.**

<table>
<tr>
<td>

Group 1

(*Alliaceae* and *Solanaceae* families)

2 Tomatoes on north-side
1 Cosmos in between
2 Peppers, 2 basil, 6 garlic in front
2 Calendula on each side

</td>
<td>

Group 2

(*Fabaceae, Chenopodiaceae, Apiaceae* and *Asteraceae* families)

6 Peas on a north-side trellis
3 Lettuce, 1 Swiss chard, 3 spinach, interplanted with the following:
9 Beets, 12 carrots
1 Cilantro, 1 parsley
2 Alyssum, 2 viola

</td>
</tr>
<tr>
<td>

Group 4

(*Fabaceae, Apiaceae, Cucurbitaceae* families)

4 cubic foot wide x 6' tall tripod planted with 4 bean seeds on north-side center
1 Dill + 1 chamomile on either side of tripod
1 Cucumber, 1 zucchini in middle
4 Marigolds in front

</td>
<td>

Group 3

(*Brassicaceae* family)

3 Kale alternated with 2 snapdragon on north-side
3 Broccoli, 2 mustard greens in middle
9 Turnips, 18 radish,
2 Nasturtium trailing over the side

</td>
</tr>
</table>

An example from my garden with 4 raised beds, 4'x8' each, incorporating companion planting and a 4-year crop rotation.

Garden plan worksheet

What vegetables and herbs do you like to cook with and eat?

What vegetables and herbs are you interested in growing?

What vegetables and herbs have you grown before? What worked well? What was challenging or unsuccessful?

Take time to consider the size of your garden. How many in-ground or raised beds will you need? What sizes?

Seed terms explained

Cultivar: A cultivated variety with specific characteristics. A cultivar name is often presented as the "variety name" after the genus and species in seed catalogs. A seed-grown cultivar can be either a hybrid or an open-pollinated variety.

GE (Genetically Engineered): The terms GE and GMO are frequently used interchangeably in the media, but they do not mean the same thing. Genetic engineering describes the high-tech methods used in recent decades on large acreage commercial crops to incorporate genes directly into an organism. These processes results in a plant that does not occur in nature.

GMO (Genetically Modified Organism): The USDA defines a GMO as an organism produced through *any* type of genetic modification, whether by high-tech modern genetic engineering or by traditional plant breeding methods. While you often hear the GE and GMO used interchangeably, they have different meanings.

Open Pollinated (a.k.a. OP): Open-pollinated varieties are seeds that result from pollination by insects, wind, self-pollination (when both male and female flowers occur on the same plant), or other natural forms of pollination.

Hybrid (F-1): An F-1, or first-generation hybrid, occurs when a breeder selects two pure lines and cross-pollinates them to produce a seed that combines desirable traits from both parents. Some traits plant breeders work to increase include disease resistance, uniformity, earliness, high nutrition, or color.

Heirloom: Heirlooms are generally defined as open-pollinated varieties that have resulted from natural selection rather than a controlled hybridization process. Some sources use seed varieties which are 50 years old, or developed prior to 1950, as an age marker to define what constitutes an heirloom variety.

Organic: "Certified Organic" on a seed packet has a distinct legal meaning. Only growers who are in compliance with all the detailed rules and regulations specified by the USDA's National Organic Program can use this label. Organic seeds are grown strictly without the use of synthetic fertilizers and pesticides, and genetic engineering is prohibited.

Pelleted: Pelleted seeds are enclosed in a round pellet made from simple clay or another inert material to bulk them up. This process makes very small seeds, such as carrots, lettuce, and onions, easier to sow and is a way to make expensive tiny flower seeds easier to see and handle.

Treated/Untreated: Seeds labeled "Treated" are generally coated with a fungicide—check the packaging for specifics about the treatment.

Safe Seed Pledge: The Safe Seed Pledge arose as a response to the release of the first genetically engineered plants in the mid-90s. Signers pledge not to buy or sell genetically engineered seeds. A list of companies that have signed the pledge is maintained by the Council for Responsible Genetics, a non-profit with a stated mission of educating the public about and advocating for socially responsible use of new genetic technologies.

Notes

Notes

4 / Garden Care
and Maintenance

YOU HAVE PLANNED AND PLANTED your garden. It's growing—now what? Even a well planned organic garden is challenged with weeds, pests, and disease. Most gardeners wonder how much to water and fertilize. We will learn how to provide ongoing care of your garden with an organic and sustainable approach to troubleshooting problems that arise.

As we learned in previous chapters, following the "right plant-right place" guideline will prevent a host of garden problems. When edible plants are planted in the appropriate season and location with adequate spacing, nutrients, and water, they are less prone to stress that results in pests, disease, and low production.

Fertilizing

As a general rule I begin my first application of organic granular fertilizer in March to prepare the garden, along with a top dressing of fresh compost or a bag of vegetable gardening planting mix that includes manure and earthworm castings. I reapply organic granular fertilizer monthly throughout the growing season, with a last application in September. Be sure to check your fertilizer package for application recommendations.

As I plant seeds and transplants in the garden, I water them with diluted liquid seaweed in my watering can. All the trace minerals it contains assist in seed germination and root growth. Beginning around July, I use an organic liquid fertilizer that promotes bloom and fruit for my fruiting plants like tomatoes, squash, and cucumbers. I continue to apply this fertilizer at 2- to 4-week intervals throughout the summer.

> *Read more about fertilizer in Chapter 1.*

Since I don't usually grow a winter garden, utilizing the winter as a time of rest for my intensively planted small garden, I don't fertilize later than September. However, if you are growing a year-round garden, you can continue with monthly fertilizer applications September through November.

Watering

There is no standard rule for how much to water your garden, as every garden is unique and different. Variables include in-ground beds, raised beds, or container gardening; soil quality and how quickly water drains; amount and intensity of sunlight; season; and type and maturity of plants.

Containers typically dry out faster than raised beds or in-ground gardens because they contain less soil. A small terra cotta container will dry out faster than a large plastic container or half wine barrel.

Gardens with soil that is well amended with compost and other organic matter should retain more water and dry out less quickly. Gardens in a full sun location with radiant heat from concrete, brick, or the side of a house will dry out quicker than gardens in partial sun or surrounded by grass and other plants.

During the hotter and drier summer months, a garden will need more watering than during the cool, wet spring. A newly sown seedbed needs to be kept evenly moist throughout the germination stage, which can mean watering twice daily. Newly planted vegetable starts have not developed root systems adequate to withstand any drought; they need more frequent watering than mature vegetable plants.

There are, however, a few watering rules that apply to all of these garden variables.

#1. Water the soil, not the plants to maximize water absorption and minimize the spread of fungal disease. This can be easily accomplished with the use of a watering wand attached to your garden hose or installing a drip irrigation system or soaker hose. Avoid overhead watering with sprinklers or a hose gun.

#2. Water your garden during the early morning. This is the coolest time of day and ensures the most water going to your soil and not lost in evaporation. During the summer in Portland, our high temperature arrives around 4:00 or 5:00pm and tends to cool overnight, sometimes as much as 30 degrees. Many fungal diseases like powdery mildew can take hold on wet plant foliage in overnight cool temperatures.

#3. Deeper less frequent watering is more efficient and effective than frequent shallow watering. When watering is shallow, light, or quick, the water stays on the garden soil surface, encouraging plant roots to remain superficial to absorb water. This in turn causes shallow rooted plants that are more prone to heat and drought stress. When watering is deeper and longer, water penetrates lower into the soil, encouraging longer, stronger plant roots that can better withstand high temperatures and dryness.

#4. The wet or dry appearance of the soil surface is not a good indicator of when to water. The soil surface may look dry and be sufficiently moist down below. Likewise, the soil surface may look wet while the lower soil is bone dry. You can easily do a simple test by sticking your finger down to the lowest knuckle into the soil. If the soil is dry at the base of your finger then it probably needs watering, if it is wet, it probably does not need watering.

I grow all my vegetables and herbs in raised beds and containers of all sizes and materials. As a general rule, during the cool spring when it doesn't rain, I water about every three days. In the peak heat of summer, I water containers daily and the raised beds every other day. By fall, when it isn't raining, I'm down to watering about every three to four days, depending on temperature. Remember, **more water is not always better.** We are aiming for the most effective, efficient watering, while conserving our precious water resource. As I am writing this summer of 2018, Oregon remains in a drought, and thoughtful watering is key to sustainability.

Weeding

The idea of weeds is purely a human construct. All plants are just plants. They are very smart, evolving entities that have widely adapted themselves to fit in just about everywhere. We define weeds as plants we don't want in our garden. Let's consider the humble dandelion. To one person it is a pesky weed ruining the look of their well-manicured lawn. To another gardener, its greens make a refreshing spring tonic or salad green, and its root is valued for its medicinal properties. Neither gardener is right or wrong, it is all a matter of your own perception.

For the vegetable gardener, a weed is a plant that is competing with desired crops for soil, nutrients, space, sunlight, and water. And, no matter what you do, there will always be weeds. Your best defense is a good offense, meaning weeding and/or laying a layer of weed block on your garden. A weed block layer can be burlap, cardboard, newspapers, or mulch.

I recommend weeding at least once a week. Catching and eliminating weeds when they are small and immature is key to successful weeding. Many weeds spread by seed, so if you can remove them before they flower and go to seed, you have won half the battle.

In my raised beds, I sit on a garden stool and pull weeds by hand. For the paths and in-ground gardens, I like to use a long-handled stirrup hoe, sometimes called a scuffle hoe, hula hoe, or oscillating hoe. Another option is the winged weeder, one of my favorite tools for my therapeutic horticulture work with seniors, people in physical rehabilitation programs, and folks with disabilities. These long-handled, light, ergonomic garden tools make weeding quick and are easy on the body.

If I am weeding weekly and catching them young, I am not so concerned about weed seeds spreading. So, the use of one of these tools to cut the leafy growth of weeds at the base is sufficient, rather than trying to remove their root systems. If weeds have not flowered and gone to seed when I cut them down with my stirrup hoe, I just leave them there in the garden to biodegrade. Never put weeds with seeds, flowers, or roots that can propagate themselves in your home composter. This will result in a serious weed situation when spreading finished compost around your yard. Typically, I toss this plant material into my curbside yard-debris bin.

If I can impart only one thing about weeds it would be that **the more regularly you remove weeds, the fewer weeds you will have over time**. This does take dedication, and it is often hard to access the time in our busy lives. But if you can view weeding as a part of the weekly chores necessary to keep your home running smoothly, like dishes and laundry, it will soon become a part of your routine. Bonus: weeding is an excellent weight-bearing exercise that burns calories, builds strength, and increases stamina, all while being surrounded in the healing power of nature.

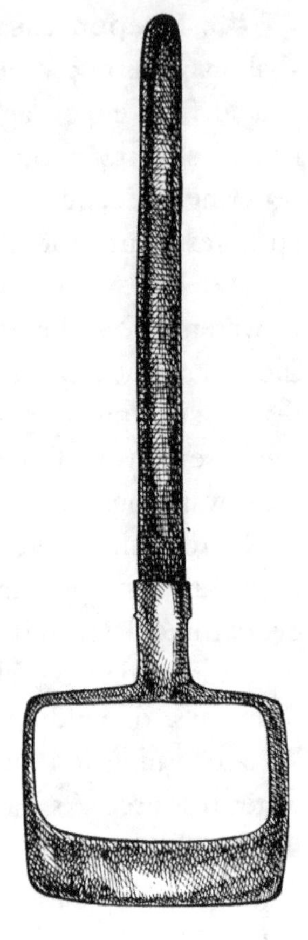

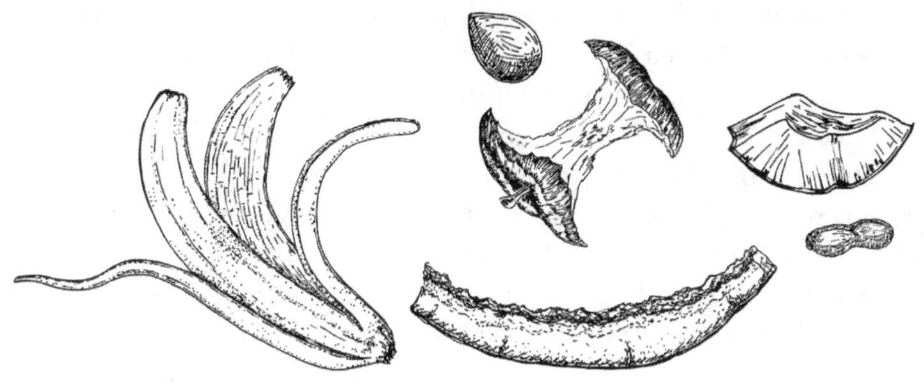

Compost

Making your own garden compost is a tried and true organic gardening technique that is cost-effective and possible in even the smallest spaces. By utilizing your own yard debris and food scraps you can create your own soil-enriching garden amendment. Making compost can seem a time-consuming and specific process. There are several composting techniques. In my own garden I use a slow, covered compost pile. I add layers of nitrogen and carbon, water it occasionally, and don't turn it. This slow composting system takes minimal effort and yields compost about twice a year.

Using a covered compost bin will discourage rodents. There are also open compost piles and trench compost techniques. Keep in mind, if you are only composting yard debris with no food and vegetable scraps, this method does not attract rodents and therefore does not need to be covered.

I think the easiest and most cost-effective covered compost bins are the black plastic composters available for sale from Metro.[3] There are also affordable compost tumblers that make it easier to turn the pile.

You can make a covered compost bin yourself by utilizing a large rubber garbage can. To transform a garbage can into a compost maker, start with a clean 32-gallon rubber garbage can with a locking lid. If the garbage can is used, you can clean it out with a biodegradable dish soap or plain vinegar and rinse completely with water.

---

3 Metro web site composter information: www.oregonmetro.gov/tools-living/yard-and-garden/composting/buy-composter

Next, drill about two dozen small holes of no larger than 1/4 inch in the bottom and sides to promote good air circulation. I like to keep this type of compost bin directly on the ground to encourage worms to enter through the holes.

When building your own compost pile, it's important to balance nitrogen and carbon materials. The ideal ratio is one part greens/nitrogen to two parts browns/carbon. Shred and break up green and brown materials prior to adding to your compost bin. The smaller the pieces, the quicker they will break down.

Avoid adding weeds with seeds and diseased plant material to the compost pile. Avocado, stone fruit pits, and walnut shells take forever to break down, so I exclude them from the compost pile. In my home compost pile, I don't meticulously turn or tend to the layers often enough for it to really heat up and kill any seeds—for this reason I don't put food scraps with seeds from winter squash, pumpkins, and melons in my compost pile. The same is true for annual flowers. If I dead-head annual flowers and toss them in the compost pile, when I spread the finished compost, it sprouts millions of unwanted seedlings!

Your compost pile should stay evenly moist, like a damp sponge, never soaking or overly wet. This overwatering will contribute to a stinky compost pile. An overly dry compost pile will take a lot longer to break down. If you find your compost pile is smelly or looks slimy, stop watering, turn the pile, and add more brown material.

If you are building a compost pile or using a compost bin that has access to the ground soil, worms will naturally find it and do the good work of composting all that waste into luscious nutritious black gold for the garden. If you are using a completely enclosed compost bin, you will need to introduce purchased worms or worms from your garden into your pile. Compost worms are the garden-variety red wigglers, not fishing bait type worms.

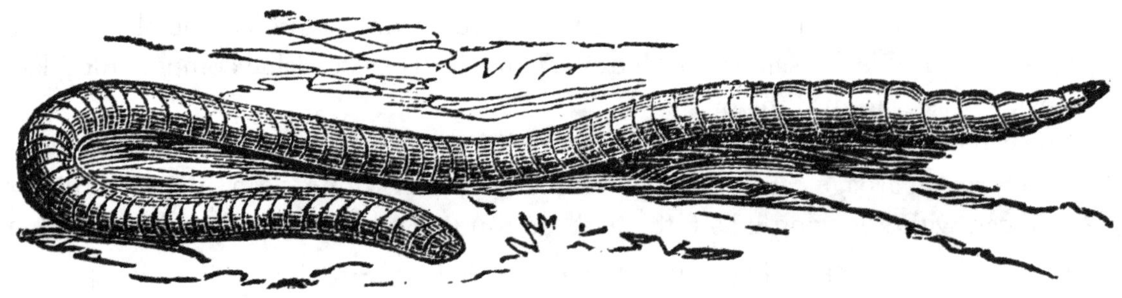

Compost ingredients

One part: Greens/Nitrogen (fresh and moist)

Fruit and vegetable scraps
Grass clippings (untreated)
Garden waste
Green pruning
Manure: chicken, pig, rabbit, goat,
sheep, horse, cow

Coffee grounds and loose leaf tea
Eggshells (rinsed)
Meals: alfalfa, kelp, blood, bone
Bat guano
Seaweed
Soil

Two parts: Browns/Carbon (dry)

Shredded newspaper (black and white
pages only)
Shredded cardboard
Brown paper bags
Shredded dry leaves
Leaf mulch
Small branches and twigs

Straw and hay
Livestock bedding
Wood chips and bark mulch
Sawdust
Pine needles
Cornstalks and sunflower stalks

Keep out of compost pile:

Avocado and stone fruit pits
Bones and meat
Cooked food
Dairy products
Cat and dog feces
Diseased or pest-infested plant material
Weed seeds
Any plant material treated with chemicals

To introduce worms into a new compost bin, I dig a few scoops of soil from my raised beds or from my finished compost pile. I find loads of healthy worms already working hard in my garden and compost pile that are happy to move into a new home.

A finished batch of compost will be a moist, loamy, black pile, rich with healthy bacteria, fungi, and other beneficial organisms. Compost can be added to raised beds, in-ground gardens, and containers. My spring-summer started compost pile is usually done in the autumn when I'm cleaning up the vegetable raised beds. After harvesting and removing all plant material, I top dress each raised bed with homemade compost and start the process all over again.

Sheet mulching

Sheet mulching or lasagna mulching is a method of composting directly in the garden bed. I have used sheet mulching extensively in a variety of garden environments during the past fifteen years. This kind of mulching, like its namesake, is made up of several layers that work together for best effect. I have used sheet mulching at the bottom of newly built raised beds and on top of existing raised beds in the fall to enrich the soil.

Utilizing sheet mulching in the fall over an unwanted existing lawn is an excellent way to create a new edible garden for springtime. Composting in place like this also means you will not need to remove pesky grass. Have you ever tried to remove sod to plant a garden? I have, and it is backbreaking work. Trust me, the sheet mulching technique is way less physically demanding, and by using natural materials from around your yard, it's very cost effective.

Sheet mulching does not have to be complicated, and I find it a rather simple way to create a new garden or enhance an existing garden rich in delicious organic matter. The basic technique is to add layers of carbon- and nitrogen-rich natural materials on soil or directly on grass to compost in place.

Sheet mulching functions much like a compost pile, and it is important to have a balance of nitrogen and carbon materials.

Here is the approximate formula I use for sheet mulching:

1. Cut down any tall vegetation and leave it in place. Poke holes in the ground with a garden fork. Sprinkle organic fertilizer high in nitrogen—like-alfalfa meal, bat guano, blood meal, or cottonseed meal. Kelp meal has tons of trace minerals, and I like to also add it. If you are using animal manure, I would spread it here. Soak this first layer well with water.

2. Add several layers of newspaper and then a layer of cardboard sheets; no need to shred either. This creates a grass-smothering and weed-blocking layer that will biodegrade. If you are using small branches, layer them on top of the cardboard. Soak this second layer well with water.

3. Add a thick layer of nitrogen materials, about 1 foot thick: loaded with fruit & vegetable scraps, green plant pruning, and grass clippings. Soak this third layer well with water.

4. Add a layer of dried leaves, and soak this fourth layer well with water.

5. Add a 1- to 3-inch layer of finished compost. This is important to introduce beneficial organisms like bacteria and fungi. Soak this fifth layer well with water.

6. Lastly, add a finishing layer to your pile. You can use topsoil or bark mulch to cover it and keep it looking tidy. Or spread on topsoil and sow cover-crop seeds directly into the topsoil. Soak this final layer well with water.

In my experience, it takes about 6 months for a sheet mulching pile to completely compost down. When I've built a sheet mulching pile in September or October it was ready to be planted by early the following spring.

Cover crops

A cover crop is a fast-growing crop that is planted primarily to keep the soil covered for a short period of time and is not for edible use. When you are ready to once again plant your garden with edible crops, the cover crop is tilled into your soil to serve as a "green manure" or added to your home compost bin. This process of turning the spent cover crop plant matter into your garden adds large quantities of organic matter to your soil. All of the nutrients contained in the cover crop plants are returned to the dirt. Organic matter will improve your soil texture and stabilize moisture content. Cover crops are great organic garden helpers, and I love using them!

Fall planting of cover crops in your edible garden can prevent weeds, erosion, and nutrient leaching during the gardening off-season. Some cover crops can even boost nitrogen in your soil. Legume family cover crops like Austrian peas, crimson clover, Dutch white clover, and fava beans are hosts to nitrogen-fixing bacteria in the soil. These bacteria extract nitrogen from the air and convert it into a form that can be used by plants.

And if that isn't enough reason to plant cover crops, some of these plants, like fava bean and oilseed radish, have long tap roots that can assist in breaking up compacted clay soil for you. Plant them in the fall, and by spring, the taproots have done their job of loosening your garden soil.

Farmers have benefited from the planting of cover crops for hundreds of years. Cover crops can be successfully utilized on a small scale for the urban gardener. The ideal time to fall plant cover crops in the Portland edible garden is September through October. This timing ensures warm enough temperatures for ideal seed germination before frosty temperatures set in.

There are several cover crop options to consider: annual ryegrass, Austria peas, buckwheat, common vetch, crimson clover, Dutch white clover, fall cereal rye, fava beans, and oilseed radish. In my experience, anything in the grass family (ryegrass, buckwheat, cereal rye) develops such a dense root mass they were virtually impossible for me to dig by hand out of my former community garden. These varieties of cover crop require a rototiller, which isn't an option for raised beds, though they still have benefits as their dense root mass is excellent for erosion protection.

I have had really good success with crimson clover, fava beans, and oilseed radish in my small scale in-ground and raised bed gardens. How I utilize cover crops in my own garden:

1. In late September harvest all annual vegetables and herbs.

2. Plant cover crop seeds by scattering them on the soil surface, raking over with a 1-inch layer of soil or compost, and watering. If squirrels are troublesome, which they are in my garden, I lay a frost blanket over the raised beds to protect the seed bed. When cover crop seeds have germinated and plants have grown a few inches tall, I remove the frost blanket.

3. Keep up weekly watering until germination if rain has not begun.

4. Wait. Cover crop plants grow all winter with no tending. If a hard frost kills them down, no worries.

5. Remove. In the spring, about three weeks before I want to plant my first vegetable crops, usually around the beginning of March, I prepare my raised beds.

First, I pull up all the cover crops by hand or with a hoe. I leave the uprooted plants laying on the soil surface, apply a dose of organic granular fertilizer directly on top of pulled-up plant material, and top with 1 to 2 inches of fresh compost. Usually, I will then cover the raised beds again with a frost blanket or layer of cardboard to keep the marauding squirrels and cats out of the fresh, unplanted soil that they cannot resist. I'm then ready to plant directly into this in about 3 weeks.

The Goddess's favorite cover crops

Crimson clover. Plant seeds in September to mid-October in the Portland edible garden. Crimson clover thrives in all types of soil and in full or partial sun. It needs moderate drainage. It quickly forms a dense green mat by winter. In June, the red flowers are a favorite of bees and beneficial bugs, though I usually have removed my crimson clover by then for spring planting edibles. Crimson clover is a favorite of mine because of its tender vegetation, making it super easy to pull and turn under into my raised bed soil. Bonus: Crimson clover is in the legume family and is a nitrogen fixing plant!

Fava bean: Plant seeds in September through October. This cover crop is another member of the legume family, related to peas, with nitrogen-fixing power. Fava beans grow tall, up to 6 feet by May. Left to maturity, they are magnificent, strong plants with striking white and black flowers. Fava beans are winter hardy to 10 degrees and can tolerate poor draining wet winter soil. They have long taproots that deeply penetrate hard garden soil, loosening it up for spring gardening. Fava beans are sturdy plants and take a little more work than soft crimson clover to remove from the garden. After pulling up the plants, use hand pruners to cut the stems into smaller pieces before spreading on the soil surface or turning under. I don't find them difficult, and they are well worth a turn in your edible garden.

Oilseed radish: Plant seeds in September through October. Oilseed radish is a member of the *Brassica* family and needs to be considered in crop rotation planning. It is a fast-growing cover crop with a long taproot. Its taproot is very helpful for breaking up and aerating compacted clay soils. Oilseed radish is not winter hardy, and a hard frost will kill the plant while the deep taproot slowly decomposes, adding organic matter back to the garden soil, leaving nothing for you to turn under in spring.

Troubleshooting pests and disease

Pests, like weeds, are a human construct. There are no good bugs or bad bug definitions in Mother Nature. All bugs are doing their unique part in the ecosystem. We gardeners define a "bad" bug as one that is eating or damaging our plants and a "good" bug as one that is adding benefits in our garden. See Chapter 3 for more information on beneficial bugs.

In the Portland area edible garden, our most common garden pests are slugs, aphids, leaf miners, and cabbage moths. If you aren't familiar with these pests and the damage they cause in the edible garden, let's help familiarize you. With this information, you will be prepared to accurately identify any pest problems. This chapter will arm you with my tips and tricks for winning the battle against the most common garden pests and disease.

For the organic gardener, the best bet against bad bugs is to attract predatory beneficial insects to the garden. Some examples of voracious predators are ladybugs, lacewings, praying mantis, and predatory wasps.

You might think that as an organic gardener, the easy answer to a pest problem is to use organic-approved pesticide sprays such as insecticidal soap, horticultural oil, neem, pyrethrin, and spinosad. The unfortunate side effect is that these are all toxic to bees and other beneficial bugs, too. The "organic" definition merely means the pesticide is derived from a plant or naturally occurring element as opposed to a synthetic chemical—not that it only kills the bad guys. Even an organic pesticide can have a devastating impact on your garden ecosystem.

As an organic gardener, using organic pesticide products is a highly personal decision you will need to make for yourself. As a steward of our planet, it is with the greatest reverence I have eliminated nearly all sprays from my garden. I will use a homemade garlic-clove spray on severe aphid infestations, and Bt in extreme cabbageworm infestations. I use both of these products sparingly, and I do so in the evening, when bees are not active, and when it is not windy, to limit their drift.

Bacillus thuringiensis (Bt) is a species of soil-living bacteria. It produces proteins that are toxic to some insects when eaten. It is an organic approved insecticide used on insect larvae, such as cabbage moths in the vegetable garden. Reportedly, it does not harm other insects like bees and ladybugs, but it is toxic to a range of butterfly caterpillars.

Slugs

Slugs are closely related to garden snails and don't have a shell. These slimy little buggers thrive in the cool, wet Portland weather. You can identify a slug presence by skeletonized leaves, shiny slime trails, and small dark feces on your plants. Slugs are most rampant throughout spring and tend to diminish in the summer heat and winter frost. Slugs come out at night and can devour an entire lettuce bed just like that! They love tender succulent plants and young seedlings. We want them somewhere else.

During the day, slugs protect themselves from dehydration and predators by hiding under rocks and pavers, under raised bed boards, under pots and containers, in cracks and crevices, and under the soil. Predators of slugs are frogs, toads, snakes, and a few types of birds. Slugs are active during mild, wet weather any time of the year in Portland.

Slugs are hermaphrodites with a 1-year lifespan, each capable of laying eggs, with greatest laying activity after the first late summer and autumn rains and again in spring. Eggs laid in October and November overwinter. You will find clusters of a dozen or more small, round, pearl-white to translucent eggs in sheltered cavities near the soil surface.

I recommend applying an organic slug bait called "Sluggo" all around the garden on bi-weekly intervals throughout autumn, winter, and spring. This product is made from naturally occurring iron phosphate and reports it has no impact on beneficial bugs, birds, and other wildlife. I have found it to be extremely effective. One downfall of this pesticide is its pellets break down quickly in water. Slugs adore the rainy season, which means more frequent application.

Copper strips can be a slug deterrent. There is some indication that a harmful chemical reaction occurs to slugs when they cross over copper. Another approach to slugs is using crushed eggshells or oyster shells scattered around your plants. Slugs will not crawl over these sharp surfaces. I do not recommend the use of diatomaceous earth (D.E.) for slugs as it has great toxicity to bees and other beneficial bugs. D.E. contains silica, which works its way under snail shells and directly onto slugs causing them to dehydrate. This can be merely unpleasant, not fatal to snails and slugs. I stand by my recommendation of crushed eggshells sprinkled around the garden soil as an economical and more effective irritant strategy.

You can also handpick slugs during the evening and morning and dispose of them as you will.

Over twenty years ago, when I was a new gardener, I tried using a homemade beer trap to cope with garden slugs. Beer traps are highly attractive to slugs because of the yeast they contain. Slugs are lured in to the beer by yeast and then drown, perhaps drunken and happy. My issue was emptying traps full of moldy beer with decomposing slugs. It was G-R-O-S-S. I've never used this method again. I also wonder if the beer traps actually attract more slugs to your garden. These are things to ponder before setting up a garden beer trap.

> **Read the book *Slug Tossing and Other Adventures of a Reluctant Gardener* by Meg Des Camp for a true and humorous account of a fellow Portland gardener.**

Aphids

Darn those aphids! I can get slugs under control, but aphids take such quick hold of both edible and ornamental plants that it can feel like a losing battle before I even start. In my vegetable garden, cabbage-family plants—kale, collard, Brussels sprouts, broccoli, and so on—are aphid favorites.

There are seemingly endless species of aphids that target specific vegetables, fruits, and ornamental plants in the garden. Aphids are tiny, soft-bodied, pear-shaped insects in shades of black, gray, brown, white, yellow, and green. Their method of destruction is to

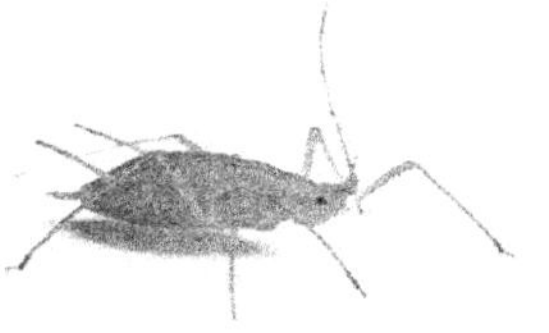

suck plant juices, so you can find them crawling on the underside of leaves and covering the new growth of vegetable plants. Heavy infestations of aphids suckering causes curled leaves and stunted plants.

And as if they aren't challenging enough as it is, get this: female aphids give birth to LIVE offspring all year without mating! How is that possible? They are like a super pest, the ultimate arch-nemesis of Portland gardeners (well, next to my neighbor's outdoor cats). Depending on climate and species, aphids produce between 2-16 generations per year. During summer and autumn, some aphid species may produce winged females and males. These mate and produce eggs for overwintering. Some adult aphids overwinter on plants if temperatures are warm enough.

Aphids secrete a large amount of honeydew nectar. Ants eat this honeydew, which is why you will observe ants protecting and "farming" aphids for their honeydew. The sticky honeydew nectar promotes development of a variety of fungal diseases including sooty mold, alfalfa mosaic, tomato yellow top, and zucchini yellow mosaic.

Don't be discouraged—if aphids are the super pest, then our organic garden superhero is the beloved humble ladybug. In addition to ladybug larvae, other natural predators of aphids are lacewing larvae and the syrphid fly. So, a great solution to an aphid infiltration is to attract and maintain a lot of ladybugs in your garden. More in Chapter 3 on how to do that.

There's also the good old-fashioned 'squish' method of battle. While I am watering the garden I will inspect leaves and if I find aphids, I squish them between my fingers and then hose my hand and the plant off with fresh water. If done daily or several times a week, this approach can be very effective in the home garden and causes the least amount of impact on your garden ecosystem.

If aphid infestation is extreme and no ladybugs are present in my garden, during the night I will apply a homemade garlic clove spray to both sides of foliage. Garlic spray has low toxicity to bees, and applying at night when bees are not active is the best way to keep them safe. If beneficial bugs are present in the aphid-infested area, I never spray. I let the good guys do their job and help out with squishing and spraying off aphids.

There is some indication that aphids are more prevalent on crops that are highly fertilized with nitrogen.[4] This is another good reason to remember, "more is not better" when it comes to fertilizer. Aphids can overwinter in weeds, or hang out there when a suitable vegetable or fruit crop is not available, so this is another good reason to stay on top of weeding around your entire garden.

---

4 Pacific Northwest Pest Management Handbooks, Oregon State University. https://pnwhandbooks.org/ insect/vegetable/vegetable-pests/hosts-pests/broccoli-brussels-sprout-cabbage-cauliflower-aphid

Garlic-Clove Spray Recipe

1 head garlic
1 tbsp. ground cloves
4 cups water

Remove individual garlic cloves and peel. Add peeled garlic, ground cloves, and one cup of water to food processor or blender. Pulse for a few minutes until garlic is completely pureed. Mix in remaining water. Place mixture in a mason jar with lid and leave to steep for 24-48 hours. Strain mixture through cheesecloth or fine mesh sieve and discard any pieces or pulp. Pour strained mixture into a spray bottle. Spray bottle can be stored in the refrigerator for two to three weeks.

Many homemade garlic spray recipes include cayenne pepper, which is toxic to bees so I do not use it. Most recipes also include some biodegradable soap to help the spray stick to plant. I omit soap in my recipe because while it is cited as a "natural" pesticide, I have no idea the toxicity to other beneficial bugs.

Leafminers

Many gardeners are not familiar with the leafminer (I wasn't!), but are familiar with how their destruction looks on leaves of beets, chard, and spinach. I frequently noticed what looked like brown mildew patches on the leaves of my beets, spinach, and Swiss chard. What I came to learn is this is the work of the leafminer that specifically seeks out this family of plants. Excessive mining renders leaves unmarketable, reduces photosynthetic capacity, and provides easy access for disease organisms. They have been challenging for me to eradicate from my garden, until recently.

Leafminer adults are small black-gray flies that emerge in spring around April or May. They lay a single or clusters of small white eggs on the underside of their host plant; the eggs hatch in about 4 days. The larvae are tiny maggots that burrow in between the leaf layers to mine tunnels. The tunnels are narrow when made by younger larvae, and larger tunnels are the work of more mature larvae. Leaves can have several maggots each. The mature larvae drop to the ground to pupate slightly under the soil surface. In 10-25 days, adult flies emerge and lay eggs for at least 3 generations a year. Leafminer pupae overwinter in the garden soil.

These facts seem like a depressing situation for any gardener who wants to grow spinach, beets, or chard. However, being knowledgeable about the leafminer life cycle is helpful in creating a pest management plan for your own organic garden. As a result of research for writing this book, I finally decreased the leafminer population in my own garden and harvested a huge quantity of healthy untarnished chard leaves. Here's how I did it.

Considering leafminer pupae overwinter in garden soil, rotating the entire beet/spinach/chard family is essential to helping control the population. However, the adult leafminer is a fly that will find the host plants in any location around your garden, so more needs to be done. Frequent careful inspection of your plant leaves will show eggs and young larvae mining leaves. Crushing the eggs and larvae or removing entire leaves is helpful in interrupting the leafminer life cycle. Leafminers' natural predator is the parasitic wasp, however, larvae are mostly protected from the parasitic wasp once they get inside the leaf tissue. Spinosad is an organic spray recommended for leafminer control, however, it has high toxicity to bees. I would not recommend it. Organic-approved neem oil has lower toxicity to bees when sprayed at night when bees are inactive and can be effective at reducing leafminer population by killing both the larvae and eggs.

Whatever approach you use, remember that leafminer adults lay eggs for at least 3 generations each year, so consistent, repeated control is needed. In my own garden, leafminers became such a problem, despite crop rotation, that I was on year two of a four-year break from growing all veggie crops in this family. As I mentioned, this year I discovered how to defeat the leafminer armed with helpful information about their life cycle and successfully reintroduced beets, chard, and spinach into my garden.

Imported cabbageworm

This pest loves to feed on all cabbage family crops and is a menace in the organic vegetable garden. The larva chews large irregular holes in cabbage leaves, bores into heads, and deposits greenish-brown feces pellets all over. The adult is a small white butterfly with two to four black spots on its wings that flits around the garden during the daytime. I often describe the cabbageworm as the drunken white butterfly because of its funny flight pattern.

Overwintering in the pupa stage on host plants, adults emerge in late April and May and lay single eggs on the undersides of outer leaves. Hatching in 4 to 8 days, larvae are small green caterpillars eating host plant leaves. Maturing in 2 to 3 weeks, caterpillars can grow to 1 inch long. Compared to other caterpillars, cabbageworms move slowly but feed voraciously. Mature larvae pupate on the host plant. In 1 to 2 weeks, adults emerge, mate, and lay eggs for 3 to 5 generations a year.

Like earlier pest investigations, we have learned that knowing the insect life cycle and interrupting it is a wise approach to planning a counter attack. Similar to my aphid intervention, I police my cabbage family plants daily for eggs and young caterpillars. Removing them before an infestation takes hold has worked well for me.

In the case of extreme infestation of cabbageworm larvae, you may employ an organic approved pesticide spray. Spinosad is recommended for cabbageworm larvae but has high toxicity to bees, so I would not use it. Bt (Bacillus thuringiensis)[5] is highly effective against imported cabbageworms and is extensively used in gardening and agriculture. It should be applied to foliage when caterpillars are young.

Please note, Bt is toxic to ALL caterpillars, not just imported cabbageworm. So, if you have planted a garden to attract local butterflies like yellow swallowtail and monarchs, it will also kill their larvae. In my garden, I keep my butterfly attractors like milkweed and Jupiter's beard away from my raised beds. I apply Bt to infested cabbage family plants sparingly, in the evening, when there is no wind, in order to minimize risk to other butterfly larvae. I find it usually only takes 1 application per year plus diligent hand-picking off to control imported cabbageworm larvae.

Keeping in mind the imported cabbageworm life cycle, and that its pupae overwinter on host plants, several interventions are helpful. Promptly harvest all crops in the autumn. Dispose of any inedible plant material in your curbside yard debris bin, not your home composter. This will deprive the overwintering generation of a safe host plant and food source.

If you are growing cabbage family crops for a winter harvest or overwintering varieties for a spring harvest, carefully inspect them for pupae. Also investigate the immediate area around host plants for pupae, remove them, and destroy.

Crop rotation of the cabbage family is very important, and a 4-year rotation is ideal. Find more on crop rotation in Chapter 3.

Disease

There are a variety of fungal diseases that can attack the Portland vegetable garden. The most common disease I see is powdery mildew, which typically attacks vegetables in the squash family, lettuce, and sometimes even leafy herbs and flowers. I have had powdery mildew plague my sage, cleome, and calendula. Generally it takes hold about mid-summer on cucumber, zucchini, pumpkin, winter squash, and melon leaves.

---

5 Bacillus thuringiensis (Bt) is a species of soil-living bacteria. It produces proteins that are toxic to some insects when eaten. It is an organic approved insecticide used on insect larvae, such as cabbage moth in the vegetable garden. Reportedly it does not harm other insects like bees and ladybugs; however, it is toxic to a range of butterfly caterpillars.

Powdery mildew is a group of soil-borne fungal diseases that loves the cool moist weather in Portland and can easily spread in the garden from soil to leaf by overhead watering. Powdery mildew can also hitch a ride on your hands, gardening gloves, and clothing. You can prevent powdery mildew by spacing plants properly to promote air circulation. Thinning plants by pruning out dense leaves of bush plants like those of zucchini and summer squash can also encourage better air circulation. By watering plants in the early morning versus the evening, foliage has time to dry during the warmest temperatures of the day. Watering by hand with a watering wand or installing a drip irrigation or soaker hose system will ensure water is reaching the soil and not splashing the leaves. Watering with a hose gun or sprinkler will splash water from soil to leaves contributing to spread of powdery mildew.

Organic-approved fungicides for powdery mildew like copper, sulfur, or neem oil can have toxicity to bees and other beneficial bugs. I would be cautious in your use of these products, as squash family plants do require pollinators to produce their fruit. I have eliminated them entirely from my organic gardening practices.

Compost tea purchased by the gallon from our neighborhood nursery has worked extremely effectively for me in preventing powdery mildew from even taking hold in the first place. Through the years I have viewed powdery mildew as an inevitable phase of the summer garden and I am sadly forced to prematurely remove my infected cucumber and squash plants. In the past few years, I have experimented with compost tea as a foliar spray and soil drench for squash family plants. Now, once a month I apply one gallon of compost tea to the leaves of and in the soil around cucumber, squash, and melon plants, and I have not developed even one spot of powdery mildew! This is such an organic gardening triumph I am overjoyed to share with you. At local nurseries, you can inexpensively purchase freshly brewed compost tea by the gallon or a package of compost tea bags to easily brew at home.

Compost tea is all-natural, has no detrimental effect on insects or wildlife, and contributes to overall soil health and fertility. I am completely won over as a loyal compost tea user.

Tomato-specific problems

Tomatoes are the number one gardening plant in the United States and I would definitely recommend them as one of the easiest and most rewarding vegetable plants for new gardeners to grow.

Tomatoes can come with a few problems that can easily be troubleshot by even the beginning gardener.

Blossom end rot

Blossom end rot can appear on immature and mature tomato fruit first as a brown circle on the base of the tomato and ultimately turning black and squishy. There are several theories about the cause of blossom end rot. The first theory is a calcium deficiency. To prevent a calcium deficiency, when planting tomatoes, apply directly into the planting hole a tablespoon each of bone meal and lime, or rock phosphate and lime if you are a vegan gardener. Later in summer, if blossom end rot is appearing on your tomatoes, you can apply a calcium-based blossom end rot spray directly onto the fruit. The second theory is inconsistent watering. Contrary to how they appear, tomatoes are actually quite drought tolerant plants. And they do appreciate watering that is consistent in frequency, duration, and quantity.

If you have experienced blossom end rot on your tomatoes, try both of these techniques and see if it will eliminate the problem in your garden. Also, remember blossom end rot does not contaminate the entire fruit. You can cut off the rotten end and still eat the rest of the tomato.

Splitting

Tomato fruits split and will develop mildew in the crack due to inconsistent watering. If tomato plants receive too much water from a summer storm or overwatering the fruit will literally burst. Again, these fruits are blemished but can still be eaten before mildew develops.

Early and late blight

Blight is a fungal disease that targets tomatoes and other *Solanum* family vegetables. Early and late blight are not common in Oregon, particularly West of the Cascades, but that doesn't mean we are immune to it. I had blight on my tomatoes in Portland about ten years ago, and so did many others. The key to coping with blight is early detection, removing and destroying all plant material, and rotating the entire *Solanum* family out of the infected garden soil area for 4 years.

You're not alone

Remember, if you run into any of these issues, you are not the only gardener who has troubles with pests, disease, weeds, plant yield, soil, and site challenges. Gardening is a lifelong learning adventure. We learn gardening by trial and error. After over twenty years of gardening, I am still learning, and I hope I never stop learning. If your garden isn't what you had hoped, don't give up. You are not a gardening failure. No one is born with a green thumb. Everyone kills plants at one time or another in their gardening careers. Read gardening books, magazines, and websites, go to lectures and garden tours, take classes and workshops, talk to other gardeners, and ask for help. There will be great gardening years and really disappointing gardening years. Take notes in a garden journal, take photos, and review them each year. And, most of all, have fun in your garden.

Notes

Notes

Notes

5 / Culinary Herbs and Edible Flowers

GROWING FRAGRANT DELECTABLE HERBS has long been a gardening passion of mine, and edible flowers are a newer favorite.

Throughout time, herbs have had a variety of uses, including culinary, medicinal, and spiritual. Generally, herbs are defined as any plant used for flavoring, fragrance, or medicine. Historically, many plants were classified as herbs, including those used to dye textiles.

After learning herb gardening basics here, please see Chapter 11 for a full description of the best herbs to grow in the Portland-area garden.

Herbs

Culinary use typically distinguishes herbs from spices based on the part of the plant that is used. An herb refers to plants used primarily for their leafy parts, either fresh or dried. A spice is a culinary product from another part of the plant such as seeds, berries, bark, roots, and fruits. Some plants are used as both herbs and spices. Dill is used for both its leaves and seeds. Cilantro is used for its fresh leaves, and its seeds are called coriander.

Culinary herbs are distinguished from vegetables in that, like spices, they are used in small amounts and provide flavor rather than substance to food.

In addition to their usefulness in cooking, many herbs are beautiful ornamental plants in the garden. Herbs are fragrant and have a wide variety of colors, textures, and shapes to delight all the senses. Every garden should include a variety of versatile and indispensable herbs.

Herbs can be divided into categories based on their growth habit. Knowing growth habits and the mature shapes and sizes of individual types of herbs will help you develop success as a gardener.

Evergreen Woody Perennial Herbs

Lavender, lemon verbena, rosemary, and sweet bay. This group of herbs can grow large like a shrub or small tree, developing thick woody stems and keeping its leaves year-round. In general, rosemary and lavender are reliably hardy in Portland. Lemon verbena and sweet bay are tender, so while technically they are evergreen woody perennial herbs, in our winter climate, the leaves can drop, and they can die.

Evergreen Perennial Herbs

Thyme. Depending on the variety, thyme can keep its leaves year-round and grows into a low mound. Due to its growth habit, it can make an excellent groundcover or trailing out of a container.

Herbaceous Perennial Herbs

Bee balm, chives, lovage, mint, oregano, Roman chamomile, sage, tarragon, and some varieties of thyme. This group of herbs varies widely in their shape and size at maturity. What they have in common is leafy growth during spring through autumn, and most die to the ground in the winter and come back in spring year after year.

Biennial Herbs

Parsley. A biennial is an herb that has a 2-year life cycle. The first-year parsley grows leaves, and in the second year it grows flowers and sets seeds.

Annual Herbs

Basil, chervil, cilantro, dill, German chamomile. An annual is an herb that has a 1-year or 1-season life cycle. It grows, typically in warmer weather, and then completely dies in the winter and does not come back. Annual herbs can, however, drop seeds and grow new plants the following year.

Next, you'll have to consider the sunlight, soil, water, and space needs of each herb. Most herbs prefer well-drained soil. Our native Portland-area soil is generally heavy on clay and receives above-average rainfall. To improve soil drainage, I amend my ground soil with organic matter like compost, mulch, and autumn leaves.

When growing herbs in containers, I use a good quality potting mix and ensure there are drainage holes.

Most herbs need full sun, 6 to 8 hours per day. Direct sunlight is needed to achieve maximum flavor and fragrance. Herbs grown in the shade become "leggy" and lack intense flavor. Leggy is a term gardeners use when a plant grows excessively tall, with few leaves, and tends to flop over. Leggy plants are usually caused by low light conditions or sometimes a lack of nitrogen.

Some herbs that can be grown in partial shade (4 to 6 hours) are chervil, lemon balm, mint, and wintergreen. Some herbs that can be grown in full shade are angelica, sweet woodruff, and yerba buena.

Most herbs do not need much fertilizer. In fact, herbs are notorious for thriving in poor soil and with neglect. Use a balanced organic fertilizer sparingly, like liquid seaweed once a month during the active growing season. Typically, I only fertilize my herb garden, both raised beds and containers, once a year at the beginning of spring. For herbs in raised beds and in the ground, I use an organic granular fertilizer directly on the soil surface and top dress with a layer of homemade compost. For herbs in containers, I use an organic granular fertilizer mixed into the potting soil at planting and transplanting time.

Watering depends on the season, the location, and the type of herb. During the wet spring, the concern is young herb plants rotting in rainy weather. In the warm dry weather of summer, herbs grown in containers dry out quicker than herbs grown in the ground or in raised beds. Most perennial herbs are established after 1 year and then are quite drought tolerant.

Herbs that do well in small containers (6-8 inch)

- Basil
- Chamomile
- Chervil
- Cilantro
- Parsley
- Savory
- Tarragon
- Thyme

Herbs that do well in medium containers (10-12 inch)

- Chives
- Dill
- Lemon balm
- Lemon verbena
- Marjoram
- Mint
- Oregano
- Sage

Herbs that do well in large containers (16 inches)

- Lavender
- Lovage
- Rosemary
- Sweet bay

Herbs in containers

Many types of herbs can successfully grow in containers, which is good news for gardeners with small spaces! You can select plastic, terracotta, glazed stoneware, or wooden containers. First and foremost, ensure your containers have drainage holes. Fill your containers with a well-draining potting soil. Never use ground soil, topsoil, or 100 percent compost in containers. Potting soil is specially formulated to promote good drainage and nutrients for plants growing specifically in containers. Select an appropriate-sized container for the mature size and growth habit of the type of herb.

Pruning

Most herbs will develop a bushier growth habit and a fuller appearance if you pinch back new growth as it emerges. This is particularly true of herbaceous perennial and annual herbs. Remembering that an annual herb has the life cycle of 1 growing season or 1 year, it will want to produce flowers and seeds for reproduction before it dies. Once an annual herb has produced flowers and seeds, it will cease leafy green growth. For example, basil flowers are lovely for attracting pollinators to the garden and make quite flavorful additions to salad; however, these flowers signal less basil leaf production. To keep your basil plants bushier and full of leaves, pinch back the flower stems all the way back to the next set of leaves. Do this at least once weekly throughout the growing season. I also do this flower tip pinching on oregano, marjoram, parsley, cilantro, mint, lemon balm, and lemon verbena.

How to pinch: Take fresh stem down to the set of leaves closest to the tip between forefinger and thumb and pinch off to remove.

Herbs that develop into a woody shrub, like rosemary or lavender, can be pruned after flowering. I also harvest entire rosemary branches as needed throughout the growing season.

Herbaceous perennials like mint, bee balm, and sage can be cut back to a few inches above the soil during fall after the first frost and during the winter. These herb plants can also be completely pruned of old dead brown growth in the spring as new growth appears.

Harvesting

Harvest herbs regularly during the active growing season to keep plants in good shape. For fresh use, harvest leaves daily as needed for cooking and tea. Morning is the best time to harvest herbs, as that's when the leaves have the most flavor. In general, herb leaves have the highest levels of oils when the blooms just begin to appear. You can harvest individual leaves or entire stems.

Preserving herbs: drying & freezing

If you are growing several types of herbs, you may want to preserve some of them in addition to harvesting as needed for your cooking. Preservation is a great idea for herbaceous herbs that die down during the winter. That way you can continue to enjoy them in your winter cooking.

> **Good candidates for drying: basil, lemon balm, lemon verbena, mint, oregano, sage, and sweet bay.**

To dry herbs, harvest their stems and shake off any dust or debris. To prevent mold and mildew, I usually I do not rinse herbs before drying. Tie several branches together tightly with twine or rubber bands and hang from the ceiling in a dry, dark location with good ventilation. If you are concerned about dust, you can cover the herb bundles by lightly draping with a paper bag or cheesecloth. Do not expose drying herbs to direct sunlight or moisture. Drying usually takes about 1 to 2 weeks, depending on the size of herb bundle and temperature.

Once dried, use your fingers to remove leaves from branches and discard the stems. Store leaves in a clean, dry, sealed glass jar in a cool dark place out of direct sunlight. I keep dried herbs for 1 year and then compost any leftovers.

Some herbs aren't very flavorful dried, such as parsley. Parsley is harvestable year-round in Portland, even winter! So, for me, it's not worth the trouble of drying and storing.

> **Good candidates for freezing: basil, chives, dill, lovage, oregano, marjoram, parsley, and sage.**

Did you know you can freeze herbs? I love using this simple preservation method for bright fresh herb flavor throughout the dreary cold winter. Herb ice cubes make excellent and surprising additions melted in winter soup, stew, gravies, and sauces.

I like to freeze individual varieties and mixtures of herbs. A favorite herbal blend to freeze is basil, oregano, and chives. Parsley and lovage pair nicely in a frozen herb cube. Sage, parsley, thyme, and lovage are a useful mixture to freeze and save for autumn recipes.

To freeze herbs in an ice cube tray, first harvest several bunches of fresh herbs—the size of a large handful—rinse, and pulse in food processor or mince by hand. Add several tablespoons of minced herbs to each ice cube section, and top off with a little water. Freeze an entire ice cube tray overnight. Remove frozen herb ice cubes and store in a labeled freezer storage bag for use throughout the winter.

Traditional basil pesto freezes perfectly for fresh flavor in the winter. Prepare your pesto recipe with fresh basil, olive oil, sea salt, garlic, and pine nuts. Omit the parmesan cheese from your recipe when freezing pesto. Add tablespoons of prepared pesto to ice cube sections, and freeze the entire tray overnight. Once frozen, remove cubes from the tray and store in labeled freezer bags. You will be amazed by how lovely, green, and sweet tasting fresh garden pesto is in the middle of a freezing winter. I love dropping basil cubes into winter minestrone soup.

To use herb ice cubes in cooking, you can add 1 cube to soup, stew, gravy, or sauce during the last few minutes of cooking. You want the herbs to melt while remaining bright and flavorful in your recipe. Overcooking frozen herbs will decrease their flavor.

Tea garden

True tea (black, oolong, white, and green) comes from the plant *Camellia sinensis*. Tea made from herbs is called tisane. Some great herbs for a tea garden in Portland:
- Basil - Genovese, cinnamon, licorice, lemon, Thai
- Chamomile - the annual German chamomile has the preferred flavor for tea
- Lavender - use flowers sparingly, they are very strong tasting
- Lemon Balm
- Lemon Verbena
- Mint - peppermint, spearmint, apple mint, chocolate mint, orange mint, ginger mint
- Monarda "Bee Balm" or "Bergamot"
- Sage - pineapple, melon, tangerine
- Thyme - English, French, orange, lemon, lime
- Yerba Buena

Herbal teas can be made from fresh or dried leaves. The general proportions are 1 teaspoon dried herbs to 1 cup water, or 2 tablespoons fresh herb leaves to 1 cup water.

When making iced teas, double the amount of herbs to preserve flavor from ice dilution.

To brew tea from fresh or dried leaves, steep herbs for 3 to 5 minutes in near boiling water, strain, and serve. Steeping herbs too long can cause tea to become bitter tasting.

One of my favorite herbal tea blends has a lemon theme, including lemon balm, lemon verbena, lemon basil, and lemon thyme. A fun floral blend includes chamomile, lavender, and rose-scented geranium flowers. Apple mint, peppermint, Monarda, and yerba buena make a tea that is crisp and bright. In my opinion, chocolate mint makes the most refreshing summer iced tea.

Edible flowers

Many flowers in the garden are not only beautiful, they are also edible! Edible flowers can add color, fragrance, and taste sensations to your culinary creations. There are edible flowers on annuals, perennials, herbs, vegetables, shrubs, and even trees.

For safety, **please keep in mind that not all flowers are edible, and some flowers are very toxic**. Never eat any flower you cannot identify with absolute certainty. While some plants with edible flowers also have leaves, roots or fruits that are edible, many edible flowers are the only part of the plant that is edible while other parts are poisonous.

Most vegetable flowers are edible. Some of the most flavorful are flowers from squash, mustard greens, arugula, broccoli, garlic, and shallot. Pea flowers and tendrils are delicious culinary treats, but do not confuse edible pea blossoms with ornamental sweet peas. Ornamental sweet pea flowers are poisonous.

Never eat the flowers from asparagus or those in the nightshade family, such as tomatoes, tomatillos, pepper, eggplant, and potatoes. These are all poisonous.

Most flowers from culinary herbs are edible, and they are the largest plant family I grow in my garden for their tasty and beautiful edible flowers. In my small space urban garden, some of my favorite plants do quadruple duty. Herbs that have leaves for culinary use, have edible flowers, attract beneficial bugs, and can be used in cut floral arrangements are my garden winners. They take top place when I am considering companion plants for vegetables. Some of these are chamomile, dill, lavender, nasturtium, rosemary, sage, and sunflowers.

Grow your own edible flowers with organic methods. Start with seeds or organic starts. Many annual edible flower plants will reseed themselves in your garden and are easy to collect and save seeds. Some of these are bachelor button, calendula, chamomile, dill, marigolds, and nasturtium.

If you buy your edible flowers as plant starts from a retail nursery or garden center and they don't explicitly state they are grown for edible use, use your best judgment. Plant nurseries grow their edible and ornamental plants differently, using a wide variety of treatments that are not always safe for consumption.

Do not harvest flowers for consumption from a garden treated with chemical pesticides, fungicides, or herbicides. If you are harvesting from a neighbor's or friend's yard, ask them what chemicals they have used. This is especially important when it comes to roses and dandelions: Both of these tend to have heavy chemical interventions.

Never eat flowers purchased from a florist. Florist flowers are grown very differently from edible plants and are usually treated with massive amounts of chemicals unsafe for consumption. The exception to this rule is cut flowers and bouquets sourced from an organic farm. Keep in mind, even if the farmer grew them organically, they still could have been treated with a chemical flower food at the flower shop. Ask to find out.

Depending on the variety, edible flowers can range in taste and fragrance from subtle to overwhelming. I find petals from calendula and viola to be very mild, adding a splash of interest, color, and delicate flavor to culinary dishes. On the other end of the spectrum, lavender flowers are very pungent, and their strong perfume flavor is best used in very small quantities.

I consider myself an edible flower explorer. One time, I was served a salad made up of only edible flowers with no other greens or vegetables, and I did not enjoy that dish. In my experience, using a few selected blossoms helps enliven a recipe. I've learned which edible flowers I enjoy by growing, tasting, and experimenting. Calendula petals are a favorite in salads and rice dishes. Violas brighten early spring salad greens. Variegated lemon thyme's tiny, pale, lavender-colored blossoms are absolutely fantastic in any dish crying out for a bright citrus flavor like salad dressing, poultry, and steamed or roasted carrots. Baked goods sing with the addition of small quantities of fragrant and strong-tasting lavender.

Bright and cheery bedding marigolds are great for deterring garden pests due to their strong smell, but I don't enjoy their large blossoms as an edible flower. However, "tangerine gem" or "lemon gem," marigolds with smaller blossoms, have a welcome citrus taste, especially in salad or dressings.

Here's a list of some edible flowers you can grow in Portland:

Angelica, *Angelica archangelica*
Anise hyssop, *Agastache foeniculum*
Apple blossom, *Malus spp.*
Bachelor Button, *Centaurea cyanus*
Basil, *Ocimum basilicum*
Bee Balm/Bergamot, *Monarda spp.*
Begonia - tuberous only, *Begonia x tuberhybridia*
Borage, *Borago officinalis*
Calendula, *Calendula officinalis*
Chamomile, *Chamaemelum nobile, Matricaria recutita*
Cherry blossom, *Prunus spp.*
Chives, *Allium spp.*
Chrysanthemum, *C. spp.*
Cilantro, *Coriandrum sativum*
Citrus blossom—lemon and orange
Citrus limonia, C. sinensis
Clover, red, *Trifolium pratense*
Daylily, *Hemerocallis spp.*
Dianthus - Pinks, Sweet William, Carnations, *Dianthus spp.*
Dill, *Anethum graveolens*
English Daisy, *Bellis perennis*
Fennel, *Foeniculum vulgare*
Fuchsia, *Fuchsia spp.*
Hibiscus (Rose of Sharon, Roselle) *H. spp., H. sabdariffa*
Hollyhock, *Alcea rosea*
Jasmine, *Jasminum officinale*
Lavender, *Lavandula angustifolia*
Lemon Balm, *Melissa officinalis*
Lemon Verbena, *Aloysia triphylla*
Lilac, *Syringa vulgaris*
Marigold, *Tagetes spp.*
Meadowsweet, *Filipendula ulmaria*
Mint, *Mentha spp.*

Mullein, *Verbascum spp.*
Nasturtium, *Tropaeolum majus*
Pansy, Violas, Johnny-Jump-Ups, *Viola spp.*
Passionflower, *Passiflora spp.*
Plum, prunes, *Prunus domestica*
Redbud, *Cercis canadensis, C. siliquastrum*
Rose, *Rosa spp.*
Rosemary, *Rosmarinus officinalis*
Safflower, *Carthamus tinctorius*
Sage, *Salvia officinalis, S. elegans*
Scented Geraniums, *Pelargonium spp.*
Snapdragon, *Antirrhinum majus*
Strawberries, *Fragaria x ananassa*
Sweet Cicely, *Myrrhis odorata*
Sweet Woodruff, *Galium odoratum*
Thyme, *Thymus spp.*
Tulip, *Tulipa spp.*
Violets, *Viola odorata*

Notes

Notes

Notes

Section Two

WINTER

6 / The Winter Garden: December, January, February

ONCE THE HOLIDAYS ARE HERE, my professional garden work slows down for the season. By the time December rolls around, our day length is much shorter, and I enjoy a well-earned break from the garden. As the winter holiday season picks up, I am busily making wreaths, swags, and garland.

Winter officially begins at the Winter Solstice on or around December 21. This is the day of the year when days are shortest and nights are longest. After the Winter Solstice, our day lengths get longer a little each day until we are back to an equal balance at the Spring Equinox in March.

Portland winters have frequent frost, wind, lots of rain, and a few snow and ice storms. Though our average temperatures are mild, keep in mind that they are an average—many days are below 30 degrees with wind chill in the 20s and 10s.

January is National Indoor Gardening Month for a good reason. Winter weather and a mostly dormant garden give me a chance to focus on growing my houseplant collection, and I have fun tending them through winter.

Quiet, cold January is also an excellent time for gardening dreams while snuggled up under blankets with a warm, fortifying cup

Average high/low temperatures and rainfall

December	46/37° F	15 days
January	46/37° F	14 days
February	51/39° F	12 days

of tea. I get out my garden journal and review the previous year, consider what didn't do well and what I really liked. I start to plan what I would like to plant this year, and I begin my garden journal for the New Year.

Make sure you are on the mailing list for the annual copies of your favorite seed catalogs. In January, I so look forward to seed catalogs coming in the mail! Some of my favorites are Territorial Seed Company, Seed Savers Exchange, Botanical Interest, Renee's Garden, Select Seeds, and High Mowing.

During January, I read, research, review, and dream big. By February, I am ready to start making a garden plan for the new year of gardening. This is an excellent time to consult a regional planting calendar. I cannot emphasize enough the value in making a garden plan and then noting in your garden journal periodically throughout the growing season. I draw out my four raised beds and start plotting vegetable, herb, and companion flowers. I use a pencil, of course, so I can make frequent changes. Keep in mind your chosen crops' size at maturity and days to maturity. You can find this information in seed catalogs, seed packets, and on transplant tags. Succession planting in spring through summer and a crop rotation system are important factors in your new year gardening plan.

See Chapter 3 for detailed monthly planting information.

I am typically not planting anything in my garden until mid to late March. Garden soil in February and March is still cold and super wet, so if planted during this time, the seeds will be slow to germinate, and many seeds or starts will just rot out in the drenched soil. Additionally, we sometimes experience a late snow in February. In Portland, there is a gardening adage, "plant peas by President's Day." In my own garden, based on years of experience, I have adopted the saying, "plant peas around or after St. Patrick's Day."

See Chapters 10 & 11 for individual vegetable and herb crop information.

In February, purchase your seeds from a local nursery or order them online from your favorite catalog. Again, having a garden plan will assist in tempering your "seed acquisition disorder," keeping you from breaking the bank!

February is a good month to assess your gardening tools and supplies. Inventory what you need, and purchase new tools, gloves, garden kneelers and stools, fertilizer, plant markers, twine, bamboo stakes, tomato cages, trellises, and containers.

If you are going to plant tomatoes, peppers, and eggplant from seed, you must start these indoors by mid- to late- February. These summer crops require heat and sunshine. Our Portland summers start late and are short lived. I always buy the starts at my local nursery in May because I don't have room indoors to start seeds and care for veggie plants. If you are fortunate to have appropriate indoor space for seed starting, much fun awaits.

Keep in mind, Portland often receives a late snow in February. Depending on the snow, rainfall, and temperature, I am beginning to prep my garden as early as mid-February for the upcoming gardening season beginning in mid-March. Wait for a dry day to pull weeds, rake, and other garden cleanup. Remember, when we walk on, shovel, or till wet soil, it causes compaction that is detrimental to our garden.

One technique to help your soil dry out faster is to cover it. If you did not cover your in-ground or raised beds in the fall, you can do so now. Covering your beds with cardboard, a frost blanket, or a tarp will help them dry out and warm up faster. This way, when the temperatures are suitable in March and April, you can begin working in your nice dry soil.

Towards the end of February, you may start seeing asparagus crowns, seed potatoes, shallot and garlic bulbs, and onion sets for sale at your local nursery. If you purchase them this early in the season, make sure you store them properly so they are still viable when planting in March. Store them in a brown paper bag in a dark, dry place to prevent mildew, sprouting, and potatoes from turning green.

Spring is really right around the corner, and some extra time spent planning and preparing now will be well appreciated later in the season during the ecstatic burst of growth and frequent gardening.

Late winter shopping list:

- ❑ Bamboo stakes - 6 to 8 feet long for building trellises and tripods
- ❑ Compost bin
- ❑ Fertilizer (organic granular for vegetables)
- ❑ Gardening gloves
- ❑ Hose
- ❑ Jute twine
- ❑ Plant markers and permanent marker
- ❑ Rubbing alcohol (for cleaning pruners)
- ❑ Seeds - cool season crops and any indoor seed starting
- ❑ Squirt bottle (for compost tea and homemade garlic spray)
- ❑ Tarp (to cover soil)
- ❑ Tomato cages - the largest size you can get, don't waste money on the little ones
- ❑ Tools - shovel, rake, spading fork, stirrup hoe, trowel, cultivator
- ❑ Watering can
- ❑ Watering wand

Notes

Notes

SPRING
MEOW!
1 MARCH

7 / The Spring Garden: March, April, May

SPRING IS SUCH A BUSY gardening season, I find it helpful to split it into early spring and late spring. This helps guide my gardening projects and planting.

March finds me really eager to get gardening again. Vegetable and herb starts begin showing up at nurseries and grocery stores. It is so exciting and tempting to buy them and plant them all right away. This may seem especially appealing if we're experiencing a warm sunny day. However, keep in mind our average last frost is between March 15 and April 15, and most vegetable crops, even cool season, will not tolerate frosty temperatures (32 degrees) at the beginning of their growing season.

March weather is wildly unpredictable with temperatures fluctuating between the 30s and the 60s with rain, hail, and wind.

Vegetable crops need not only higher daytime temperatures, they also need warmer soil temperatures, and they need the soil to dry out. In cool, waterlogged soil you'll find that tubers, crowns, and roots will rot, seeds will not germinate, and tiny starts and seedlings will be stunted and struggle to grow. In general, as March proceeds into April, we experience more favorable planting conditions. It really varies year to year how soon to begin planting. Planting early doesn't always give

Average high/low temperatures and rainfall		
March	56/41° F	14 days
April	61/44° F	12 days
May	67/49° F	9 days

you a jump-start, it often results in stressed, stunted, and dead plants. Consistent monitoring of the daily and weekly forecast is indispensable for the Portland gardener.

At the beginning of March, I have two projects to prepare the garden: If in the autumn I planted cover crops, now is the time I gently pull them out and turn them into the soil very lightly. **As you know, I advocate no-till gardening methods. I do not use a rototiller or turn the soil very deeply.** I lay pulled-up cover crops on the top of the garden soil, add a dose of granular organic fertilizer, and cover with a fresh layer of compost. I find two weeks is sufficient time to break down and be ready to be planted into.

> *More information on cover crops and sheet mulching in Chapter 4.*

If I did sheet mulching in the fall, I remove any weeds with my hoe, and I take my garden fork and gently poke around to see how the pile progressed during the winter. I might also add a dose of granular organic fertilizer and a fresh layer of compost at this time.

Rain is still quite heavy in March, and as you have learned in previous chapters, walking on, working in, and planting in wet soil destroys soil structure and causes detrimental compaction. So now would be an ideal time (if you haven't done it already) to cover your garden soil with a tarp, a frost blanket, or cardboard to help it dry out a little.

I do this preparation at the beginning of March so that as soon as temperatures warm and the soil dries out a little, I am ready to jump into planting!

March to-do list

- ❑ Prepare your garden beds by pulling weeds, removing winter debris, apply fertilizer, top dress with compost, and use a spading fork to gently work into the soil. Turn under fall-planted cover crops. Cover your beds back up with cardboard, tarp, or frost blanket until you are ready to plant or they will sprout new weeds and attract cats and squirrels.

- ❑ Install drip irrigation or soaker hoses now before planting.

- ❑ Build tripod or trellis with bamboo stakes and jute twine for peas to climb.

- ❑ Plant vegetable starts and seedlings after March 15: artichoke, Asian greens, broccoli, cabbage, chard, collards, fava beans, kale, leeks, lettuce, mustard greens, peas, salad greens, scallions, and spinach.

- ❑ Plant seeds directly in the garden: arugula, Asian greens, lettuce, kale, mustard greens, peas, radish, scallions, spinach, and turnips. **Remember: soil can still be quite cold, so consult soil temperature needs of each crop and consider warming the seedbed by covering it with a frost blanket or constructing a cold frame or low tunnel. You can purchase a soil thermometer at your local nursery or garden center.

❑ Plant asparagus crowns, garlic cloves, horseradish roots, potato tubers, onion sets, and sunchoke tubers.

❑ Plant cool season herbs like cilantro and chervil from seed or starts/seedlings. Plant annual herbs from seeds or starts/seedlings: chamomile, dill, and parsley.

❑ Plant perennial herbs from starts including: chives, feverfew, lavender, lemon balm, lovage, marjoram, mint, oregano, rosemary, sage, winter savory, and thyme.

❑ Apply organic slug bait all around the garden on a 2- to 3-week re-application schedule.

April to-do list

❑ If you did not prepare your garden beds in March, do so now by following instructions in the March to-do.

❑ If you top-dressed the garden with the first application of organic granular fertilizer in March, begin monthly applications in April.

❑ Continue to apply organic slug bait around the garden at 2- to 3-week intervals.

❑ Throughout this month, plant:
Asian greens from seeds or starts
Beets from seeds
Broccoli/broccolini/broccoli raab from starts
Brussels sprouts (plant now for fall harvest)
Cauliflower from starts
Carrots from seeds (I usually start around April 15)
Collards from seeds or starts
Florence fennel from seeds or starts
Kale from seeds or starts
Leeks from starts
Lettuce from seeds or starts
Mesclun mix from seed
Mustard greens from seeds or starts
Peas from seeds or starts
Radicchio from seeds or starts
Radishes from seeds
Salad greens - arugula, cress, endive, escarole, mache, purslane from seeds
Scallions from seeds or starts
Spinach from seeds or starts

Swiss chard from seeds or starts
Turnip from seeds

☐ Plant potatoes from tubers, horseradish from roots, and sunchokes from tubers. The ideal time for planting asparagus crowns is February and March, though you could try planting at the beginning of April if they are still available.

☐ Most of the allium family is typically fall-planted. However, onion plants sold in bunches like 'Walla Walla' sweet onions are best planted in April. In April you can plant scallions from seed or starts, leeks from starts, onions from sets or bunches, shallots from cloves, and garlic from cloves or starts.

☐ The only cool season bean variety you can begin planting around April 15 are runner beans like 'Scarlet Runner.' Plant runner beans by seed as soon as April 15; hold off on all other beans until the warmer weather in May.

☐ Herbs in April: Plant cool season annual herbs like chervil and cilantro from seeds or starts. Plant hardier annual summer herbs like dill and German chamomile. Wait on planting warm season summer herbs like basil and shiso. Plant all perennial and biennial herbs now.

☐ April is a great time to plant companion flowers in the vegetable garden, and summer blooming annual flower plants start arriving at nurseries. Look for alyssum, calendula, cleome, cosmos, marigolds, nasturtium, and snapdragons. Zinnia starts can be slow to arrive to nurseries, sometimes as late as May. On April 15, you can begin direct seeding sunflowers in the garden.

☐ As tempted as you may be in April, please hold off on planting warm season summer vegetables until May when both night and day temperatures are consistently warm enough. This means you still have to wait on basil, beans, celery, corn, cucumbers, eggplant, melons, peppers, pumpkins, summer squash, sweet potatoes, tomatoes, tomatillos, winter squash, and zucchini.

May to-do list

☐ Continue monthly top-dressing garden beds with organic granular fertilizer.

☐ Continue to apply organic slug bait around the garden at 2- to 3-week intervals.

☐ Purchase tomato cages, bamboo stakes, and tripods to install for support when planting warm season vegetables.

☐ Purchase frost blankets, walls-of-water, and cloches. Be prepared to monitor night temperatures for drops below 55 degrees, and cover tender plants overnight.

❑ Continue planting these cool season vegetables through May: Asian greens, beets, broccoli, Brussels sprouts, cauliflower, cabbage, carrots, collards, fennel, kale, kohlrabi, lettuce, mustard greens, radish, salad greens, scallions, spinach, and Swiss chard.

❑ Begin planting these warm season vegetables after May 15 or when night temperatures are consistently above 55 degrees:

❑ Beans (seed)

❑ Celery (starts)

❑ Corn (seeds or starts)

❑ Cucumbers (seeds or starts)

❑ Eggplant (starts)

❑ Melons (starts)

❑ Peppers (starts)

❑ Pumpkins (seeds or starts)

❑ Summer Squash (seeds or starts)

❑ Sweet Potatoes (slips or starts)

❑ Tomatoes (starts)

❑ Tomatillos (starts)

❑ Winter Squash (seeds or starts)

❑ Zucchini (seeds or starts)

❑ Continue planting all perennial herbs. Continue planting all hardy annual herbs and a last round of cool season annual herbs like cilantro and chervil. Begin planting basil when night temperatures are consistently above 55 degrees.

❑ Continue planting seed potatoes through May.

❑ Harvest cool-season veggies planted in March and April as well as overwintering veggies planted the previous fall. Sugar snap and snow peas are most flavorful and tender when harvested small. Fall-planted garlic is now producing dramatic looking tasty scapes you can harvest and sauté. Utilize cut-and-come-again harvest method for mesclun mix and smaller salad greens. Keep kale, collards, chard, spinach, and lettuce regularly harvested to prevent bolting and bitter taste. The young smaller leaves are more tender and sweet tasting. If warm temperature spikes are predicted, harvest whole heads of broccoli, and leave the stem intact to produce side shoots.

❑ May continues to be an excellent month to plant companion flowers in the vegetable garden, and summer blooming annual flower plants are widely available at local nurseries. Look for alyssum, calendula, cleome, cosmos, marigolds, nasturtium, snapdragons, and zinnia.

❑ Plant sunflowers by direct seeding in the garden. Other quick-germinating annual flower seeds to plant in May are cosmos and nasturtium.

Early spring shopping list

❑ Annual companion flowers (transplants) as they become available: alyssum, pansy, viola

❑ Asparagus crowns, garlic cloves, horseradish roots, potato tubers, onion sets, shallot cloves, strawberry crowns, and sunchoke tubers

❑ Bamboo stakes 6 to 8 feet long for building trellises and tripods—peas and runner beans will need them

❑ Compost and soil amendments like sand, manure, etc.

❑ Drip irrigation or soaker hose, if using, to install prior to planting

❑ Fertilizer (organic granular for vegetables)

❑ Herb plants, early/cool season annuals: chamomile, chervil, cilantro, dill, parsley

❑ Herb plants, perennials: chives, feverfew, lavender, lemon balm, lovage, marjoram, mint, oregano, rosemary, sage, savory sweet bay, and thyme

❑ Jute twine

❑ Liquid seaweed (for seeds and transplants)

❑ Onion bunches (like 'Walla Walla Sweets')

❑ Organic slug bait

❑ Plant markers and permanent marker for seed beds

❑ Seeds: cool season crops like arugula, chervil, cilantro, lettuce, peas, radish, runner beans, salad greens, scallion, spinach, and turnip

❑ Vegetable starts for the cool season (consult full list in March and April to-do lists)

❑ Tarp (to cover soil)

Late spring shopping list

- ❑ Annual companion flowers (transplants) as they become available: alyssum, calendula, cleome, cosmos, marigolds, nasturtium, snapdragons, and zinnia
- ❑ Bamboo stakes, 6 to 8 feet long, for building tripods and trellises for pole and runner beans
- ❑ Compost tea or compost tea bags
- ❑ Cool temperature protection for warm season veggies: cloche, frost blanket, and/or wall-of-water
- ❑ Fertilizer (organic granular for vegetables)
- ❑ Herb plants, cool and warm season annuals: basil, chamomile, chervil, cilantro, dill, parsley
- ❑ Herb plants, perennials: chives, feverfew, lavender, lemon balm, lovage, marjoram, mint, oregano, rosemary, sage, savory sweet bay, and thyme
- ❑ Jute twine
- ❑ Liquid seaweed (for seeds and transplants)
- ❑ Onion bunches (like 'Walla Walla Sweets')
- ❑ Organic slug bait
- ❑ Plant markers and permanent marker for seed beds
- ❑ Potato tubers
- ❑ Seeds for annual flowers: cosmos, nasturtium, sunflowers
- ❑ Tomato cages—get the largest size you can find, you will need it!
- ❑ Vegetable seeds for cool and warm season: arugula, beets, bush beans, carrots, corn, cucumber, lettuce, pole beans, radish, runner beans, salad greens, scallion, spinach, squash, and turnip
- ❑ Vegetable starts for the cool season and the warm season (consult full list in May to-do lists)

Notes

Notes

SUMMER

8 / The Summer Garden: June, July, August

SUMMER IS A MULTIFACETED SEASON in the garden. The first official day of summer is the Solstice on or around June 21. At the beginning of June, if the spring has been slow to warm up, I plant my warm season crops like basil and cucumbers. I continue succession planting of lettuce, carrots, and annual herbs like dill and chamomile. Throughout the month of June, I harvest the last of the cool season spring crops like spinach, arugula, mache, cilantro, chervil, and peas before the hot summer temperatures cause them to bolt.

Bolting is when a plant prematurely abandons leaf growth, sends up a flower stalk, and quickly goes to flower and seed. In fluctuating or prolonged warm or hot temperatures, a plant may focus on seeds and reproduction as a survival mechanism. When cool season annual vegetables like lettuce or herbs like cilantro bolt, they no longer produce leaves, and the leaves that remain taste bitter.

By the time the first of July rolls around, I am usually quite exhausted from nonstop planting and gardening projects the prior three months. When the warm summer begins, I am eager to put my feet up and enjoy a glass of iced tea in the garden. Yet this is usually the time my bountiful, colorful

Average high/low temperatures and rainfall		
June	73/53° F	5 days
July	80/51° F	2 days
August	80/58° F	2 days

garden is undermined by fungal diseases like powdery mildew, attacks by menacing aphids, and vigorous weeds. And let's not forget, we likely won't see rain again until September, so consistent early morning watering demands my attention lest the happy garden begins to wilt and suffer.

What's a gardener to do? An ounce of prevention with daily attention to the garden goes a long way. And there is still time for a leisurely glass of iced tea admiring the beauty of a well-cared for garden.

> *See Chapter 4 for more information on pests, diseases, and weeds.*

It might feel counterintuitive to consider July and August as months for planting an edible garden for fall and winter harvest. You might be saying "are you kidding me, Jolie?" I'm not! Our average first frost is anywhere between October 15 and December 15, and you want all fall and winter crops to be at harvestable maturity by this date. So looking at a seed packet of broccoli with 75 days to maturity, it needs to be direct seeded in the garden around the first week of August to be harvestable in mid-October.

> *See Chapter 1 for frost date and growing season information.*

Did you save room in your edible garden for a round of fall/winter planting in July and August? If you are like me, nope! In July and August my three raised beds are packed with tomatoes, cucumbers, beans, summer squash, summer lettuce, and basil. When these crops are fully harvested in September, it will usually be too late to plant kale, broccoli, beets, turnips, and cool-season friends for a fall and winter harvest. What is an urban gardener to do?

It might take some trial and error, but you will need to prioritize which seasons and crops are important to you. That way, with annual garden planning, you'll save space for year-round crops. Since I garden so intensively in four raised beds, one reserved exclusively for herbs, I garden and harvest during March through October. I give my garden beds a much-deserved winter rest in November through February.

Also consider a later planting of the fall/winter garden in September, and utilize season extension techniques like frost blankets, low tunnels, cold frames, and cloches.

The number one garden task during the summer is watering. Consistent early morning deep watering done with a watering wand promotes a healthy garden. Efficient and effective watering is also accomplished with a soaker hose or drip irrigation. How often you water will depend on the depth, drainage, and water retention of your soil. Containers and more shallow raised beds will need a more frequent watering than in-ground and taller raised beds. Terra cotta pots dry out quicker than plastic and glazed ceramic.

On average I water my raised beds every 2-3 days during the peak heat of summer. The containers usually need daily watering. Again, there is no set rule for summer watering, it is highly variable depending on the individual garden.

If you're thinking that spraying your garden with a hose is good enough and you don't need to buy a wand or set up a ground-level watering system, remember that fungal diseases like powdery mildew are often spread by this kind of overhead watering. Powdery mildew tends to take hold at the beginning of summer, spreading among the leaves of squash, cucumber, melons, pumpkins, lettuce, salad greens, and some annual flowers like calendula.

Use of compost tea at 3- to 4-week intervals throughout the summer can be extremely helpful at preventing and treating powdery mildew. I use compost tea as both a foliar spray and soil drench. Compost tea by the gallon can be purchased at local nurseries. You can also purchase compost tea bags to easily brew yours at home.

To foliar spray, spray both sides of every leaf. Drenching means pouring 1 to 2 cups of compost tea directly on soil around squash family plants.

Along with powdery mildew, summer is the season of the aphid. Ugh, those nasty little aphids sucking the life out of vegetables, fruit, herbs, and flowers. Taking a daily morning stroll of my garden to closely inspect the aphid's favorite plants results in early detection—in my experience, they tend to target kale, collards, broccoli, and Brussels sprouts. When aphid infestation is relatively small, I will squish them off each plant with my fingers and then rinse with water.

> *See Chapter 4 for more aphid-busting tips.*

My morning garden inspection also includes pinching flowers off of basil, moving growing tomato stems back into their cages, plucking weeds, and assessing what is ready to harvest. I observe my tomatoes for any signs of splitting or blossom end rot. Keep harvesting those pole beans daily, while they are pencil thin, for best flavor and continued production. The same goes for frequent harvesting of zucchini and summer squash. Don't wait until they are the size of a football to harvest, as they lose their peak flavor and fill up with more seeds than flesh.

There is usually always an abundance of bees in my garden, but it is a good idea to confirm pollination is happening on squash family plants: cucumber, zucchini, summer squash, winter squash, melons, pumpkins, and gourds. If the plants have flowers, and young fruit is dropping off the plant, lack of pollination can be the culprit. As you have learned, you can encourage pollinators by companion-planting veggies with flowers and utilizing no-spray organic gardening methods. If this isn't enough, you may need to hand-pollinate your squash plants. You can hand pollinate your squash family plants by first identifying the male flowers and female flowers. Inside the male flowers there is a small cone shape covered in pollen. Inside the female flowers is a flat disc shape covered in pollen. Take a clean paintbrush or cotton swab, dip into the male flower and coat with pollen, and then apply the pollen inside the female flower. Repeat daily to pollinate every female flower.

The bounty of the summer garden is just around the corner. Now is a great time to learn food preservation techniques such as canning, freezing, and dehydrating. Educate yourself and make a plan now so that you don't waste a morsel from your garden's bounty—learn from a friend, take a class, or find a good book on food preservation.

June to-do list

- [ ] During the first 2 weeks of June, you can continue to plant warm season crops like basil, beans, corn, cucumbers, eggplant, melons, peppers, pumpkins, summer squash, sweet potatoes, tomatoes, tomatillos, winter squash, and zucchini. With the exception of beans from seeds, plant transplants. Purchase the largest plants possible. Gallon-size plants begin arriving at nurseries at the end of May.

- [ ] During the first 2 weeks of June, you should plant only summer varieties of lettuce. Look for heat-tolerant bolt-resistant varieties like: buttercrunch, drunken woman frizzy headed, Tom Thumb, and valmaine. In general, French crisp, or Batavia, varieties of lettuce are good summer lettuces. Seed catalogs and plant tags will indicate heat-tolerance and summer appropriateness.

- [ ] Continue your succession planting of beets, bush beans, carrots, chamomile, dill, and radishes from seed.

- [ ] It is still not too late to plant summer-flowering annuals as companion plants in the veggie garden. Look for transplants of alyssum, calendula, cosmos, marigolds, nasturtium, and zinnias. You want to get these planted by the end of June, before the summer heat really sets in.

- [ ] Transplant Brussels sprouts, and plant celeriac/celery root, leeks, parsley root, and parsnip seeds for a fall/winter harvest.

- [ ] Apply compost tea as a foliar spray on squash family plants, and soil drench every 3 to 4 weeks. Increase frequency of applications if powdery mildew is taking hold and spreading.

- [ ] Establish and maintain a consistent watering routine.

- [ ] Squish and hose off aphids. Apply organic slug bait about once a month, if needed. Inspect for caterpillars and remove from Brassica family plants.

- [ ] Frequently harvest kale, collards, lettuce, spinach, chard and other greens to prevent bolting.

- ❏ Harvest the last of sugar snap, snow, and shelling pea varieties. Prepare for these plants to be done producing with the July heat. You can replant in late August or early September for a fall harvest.

- ❏ Top dress garden beds and containers with organic granular vegetable fertilizer on 30-day intervals.

- ❏ During the month of June, pinch off flowers from tomato, cucumber, pepper, eggplant, melon, and pumpkin plants until they have developed larger more vigorous plants. Usually this happens by the end of June. Continue pruning tomato plants by pinching off the sucker shoots in between stems and main branches.

July to-do list

- ❏ Continue consistent early morning watering routine.

- ❏ Top dress garden beds and containers with organic granular vegetable fertilizer on 30-day intervals.

- ❏ Begin using a liquid "bloom & fruit" fertilizer with a higher middle number of phosphorus (remember N-P-K in Chapter 1). Full fertilizer information can be found in Chapter 1 and in Chapter 4. Use this fertilizer for tomatoes, peppers, cucumbers, melons, pumpkins, summer squash, eggplant, winter squash, and zucchini.

August to-do list

- ❏ Continue watering, granular organic fertilizer, and compost tea routines from July.

- ❏ By now, the summer garden should be bursting with warm-season crops. Be sure to frequently harvest basil, beans, cucumber, eggplant, peppers, summer squash, tomatoes, tomatillos, and zucchini. If you have more than you can eat, preserve it, give to friends, or consider donating to your local food bank or pantry. Delicious, nutritious home-grown organic vegetables should never go to waste!

- ❏ August is the big month for planting the fall/winter vegetable garden. A lot of crops have to go into the ground now to ensure harvest by October. From seed: beets, carrots, kohlrabi, lettuce, radish, turnip, and salad greens like endive, escarole, mache, mesclun mix, radicchio. From transplants: broccoli, cabbage, cauliflower, collards, fennel, kale, leeks, lettuce, mustard greens, peas, spinach, swish chard.

Summer shopping list

- ❑ Compost tea - premade gallon or tea bags
- ❑ Squirt bottle to apply compost tea
- ❑ Organic liquid bloom/fruit fertilizer
- ❑ Watering can to apply diluted liquid fertilizer
- ❑ Blossom end rot spray (liquid calcium) if needed
- ❑ Harvest basket or tub
- ❑ Seeds for vegetable crops for fall/winter harvest
- ❑ Transplants for vegetable crops for fall/winter harvest

Winter harvest planting guide

Crop	Sowing Seeds	Planting Starts/ Transplanting	Harvest
Arugula	Direct seed in garden August through September	Transplanting not recommended	30-40 days from planting. Harvestable all winter down to 10 degrees
Beets	Direct seed in garden July through August	Transplanting not recommended	60 days from germination. Harvestable down to 20 degrees
Broccoli Fall/Winter varieties (includes crown broccoli, sprouting broccoli, broccolini, and raab/rapini)	Direct seeding not recommended	Plant starts in garden mid-July through August	60-90 days from transplanting. Harvestable down to 30 degrees
Broccoli - overwintering varieties	Direct seeding not recommended	Plant starts in garden late August through early September	Harvest the next February through March

Crop	Sowing Seeds	Planting Starts/ Transplanting	Harvest
Brussels Sprouts	Direct seeding not recommended	Plant starts in garden May through June	Approximately 120 days from transplanting. Harvest begins in October and lasts all winter. Harvestable down to 28 degrees
Cabbage	Direct seeding not recommended	Plant starts in garden mid July through August	60-90 days from transplanting. Harvestable down to 28 degrees
Carrots	Direct seed in garden July through August	Transplanting not recommended	60-90 days from germination. Harvestable all winter down to 5 degrees
Cauliflower	Direct seeding not recommended	Plant starts in garden July through August	60-90 days from transplanting. Harvestable down to 10 degrees
Chinese Cabbage	Direct seeding not recommended	Plant starts in garden mid-July through August	60-70 days from transplanting. Harvestable down to 20 degrees
Chervil	Direct seed in garden or containers in late August through September	Transplanting not recommended	30 days from germination. Harvestable down to 30 degrees
Cilantro	Direct seed in garden August through September	Plant starts in garden August through October	60 days from germination and 30 days from starts. Harvestable down to 28 degrees
Collards	Direct seed in garden mid-July	Plant starts in garden August (preferred method)	70 days from germination and 40 days from starts. Harvestable all winter down to 10 degrees

Crop	Sowing Seeds	Planting Starts/ Transplanting	Harvest
Endive/ Escarole	Direct seed in garden in August	Plants starts in garden August through September	60 days from germination and 30 days from starts. Harvestable down to 30 degrees
Fava Beans - an overwintering crop	Direct seed in garden September through October	Transplanting not recommended	Harvest the following spring into early summer
Florence Fennel	Direct seed in garden the beginning of August	Plant starts in garden mid-August through September	Harvest 70 days from germination and 30-50 days from starts. Harvestable down to 30 degrees
Garlic - an overwintering crop	Plant garlic cloves in garden September through October	N/A	Harvest the next spring into early summer
Kale	Direct seed in garden in mid-July	Plant starts in garden August (preferred method)	Harvest 70 days from germination and 40 days from starts. Harvestable all winter down to 10 degrees
Kohlrabi	Direct seed in garden mid-July through August	Transplanting not recommended	60 days from germination. Harvestable all winter down to 5 degrees
Leeks	Direct seeding not recommended	Plant starts in garden June through beginning of July	90 days from transplanting. Harvest all winter down to 5 degrees
Lettuce	Direct seed in garden August through September	Plant starts in garden mid-August through September	50 days from germination and 30 days from transplanting. Depending on variety harvest most of winter down into 20s

Crop	Sowing Seeds	Planting Starts/ Transplanting	Harvest
Mache/Corn Salad	Direct seed in garden August through September	Transplanting not recommended	50 days from germination. Harvest all winter down to 5 degrees
Mustard Greens	Direct seed mid-July through August	Plant starts in garden August through September (preferred method)	60 days from germination and 30 days from transplant. Harvest all winter down to 5 degrees
Pac Choi	Direct seed in mid-July	Plant starts in garden in August (preferred method)	60 days from germination and 30 days from transplant. Harvestable down to 20 degrees
Parsley	Direct seeding not recommended	Plant starts in garden August through September	30 days from transplanting. Harvestable all winter long
Parsnips	Direct seed in garden June through July	Transplanting not recommended	120 days from germination. Harvestable all winter down to 5 degrees
Peas	Direct seed in garden mid to late July	Plant starts in garden August	70 days from germination and 50 days from transplanting. Harvestable down to 15 degrees
Radicchio	Direct seed in the garden July	Plants starts in garden August (preferred method)	80 days from germination and 60 days from transplanting Harvestable down to 20 degrees
Radishes	Direct seed in garden August through September	Transplanting not recommended	20-30 days from germination. Harvestable down to 20 degrees
Rutabagas	Direct seed in garden in July	Transplanting not recommended	90 days from germination. Harvestable down to 20 degrees

Crop	Sowing Seeds	Planting Starts/ Transplanting	Harvest
Scallions	Direct seed in garden July through August	Plant starts in garden August through September	50 days from germination and 30 days from transplanting. Harvestable all winter down to 10 degrees
Shallots - an overwintering crop	Plant shallot bulbs in garden September through October	N/A	Harvest next spring into early summer
Spinach	Direct seed in garden July through August	Plant starts in garden August through September (preferred method)	50 days from germination and 30 days from transplanting. Harvestable all winter down to 10 degrees
Swiss Chard	Direct seed in garden in July	Plant starts in garden in August (preferred method)	60 days from germination and 40 days from transplanting. Harvestable all winter down to 5 degrees
Turnips	Direct seed in garden July through August	Not recommended	60 days from germination. Harvestable down to 20 degrees

Notes

Notes

Notes

AUTUMN
SCHOOL BUS

9 / The Autumn Garden: September, October, November

AUTUMN OFFICIALLY BEGINS at the Autumn Equinox on or around September 21 of every year. September rolls in after a busy summer, and I can feel a change is in the air. Although September can feel like an extension of summer, the garden begins looking different, and I know that in a few months, we will quickly begin the transition to winter.

Autumn is my favorite season, and its equinox is the second of three Celtic harvest festivals we celebrate in my family. I love the seasonal color change, the cooler weather, the return of the rain intermixed with warm sunny days, and the bounty to harvest in the garden. September is the end of local peaches, nectarines, and plums and the glorious beginning of local apples and pears. In the backyard edible garden, we are harvesting the summer's generosity of vegetables and herbs. Summer-planted vegetables for a fall and winter harvest are beginning to reach maturity.

Autumn weather from September through November can be extremely varied. Rain, hail, wind, and thunderstorms all return in the autumn.

Historically, our average first frost date in Portland is October 15. Due to changes in our climate, however, sources now site anywhere between November 15 through

Average high/low temperatures and rainfall		
September	75/54° F	5 days
October	63/48° F	9 days
November	52/41° F	15 days

December 15 as our average first frost date. As I am writing this book in 2019, I harvested lettuce until after Thanksgiving 2018, and we did not receive our first frost until January 1, 2019. I predict a trend that we can garden later into the season, though Mother Nature may have other ideas about autumn weather.

Frost occurs on or below 32 degrees Fahrenheit. Most vegetables will not grow in frost. Many of our summer vegetables, like tomatoes, cucumbers, and peppers, will become stunted and stop producing when temperatures dip below 50 degrees. The taste of some cool season vegetables, such as Brussels sprouts and parsnips, improves with a light frost.

For the urban edible gardener in Portland, there are a few guiding principles to remember about the autumn season. As we approach the Autumn Equinox on September 21, the day and night lengths are equal. From here until the Winter Solstice on December 21, our day lengths continue to get shorter, and night lengths continues to get longer. This means fewer hours of sunlight to help plants grow. Additionally, during autumn and winter, the earth is farther away from the sun, and we're not getting summer's direct powerful sunlight. In terms of edible gardens, temperatures might still be ideal for cool season crops; however, the day length and strength of sun are not ideal for vigorous growth.

Many cool season vegetables, like kale, broccoli, Brussels sprouts, and cabbage, will not continue to grow in the cooler temperatures, but they will tolerate the cooler weather and therefore are harvestable throughout the winter. Ideally, you want your vegetables for a fall and winter harvest to be at mature size by our first frost, somewhere around October 15. The guiding tip for a fall and winter garden is to look at the days to maturity listed on a seed packet or plant tag that comes with a transplant. Then count back from October 15 to determine its recommended planting date. For example, if a broccoli start has a tag that says 60 days to maturity, then plant it in your garden by August 15.

Typically, we plant crops for a fall and winter harvest during the mid-summer season (see Chapter 8). If you did not get fall and winter crops planted during the summer, don't despair, there are still some gardening projects for you to start! And, given our shift in average first frost date and warmer autumn temperatures, I think we can experiment with planting vegetables even later into September for a fall and winter harvest.

Salad greens

Some crops that we can still plant in September are quick growing salad greens like arugula, mache, cress, and mesclun mix. Direct seed these in containers, raised beds, or in-ground gardens throughout September. They should be harvestable within about 1 month. Beware the menacing squirrel in your fall gardens. This critter is busy burying nuts all over your garden, and she loves fresh, soft, uncovered soil. She will wreak havoc on new seedbeds and uncovered garden soil. If you are planting seeds for salad greens, cover them with netting, frost blankets, or other physical barriers to thwart squirrels. Be sure to continue applying slug bait at 2-week intervals to prevent them from munching away your tender salad greens. Harvest salad greens as needed through October and November until frost sets in.

Garlic and shallots

Garlic and shallots prefer being planted in the fall. Here in Portland, we plant them in September and October. They need the cooler weather for root growth before the cold of winter sets in. In very early spring, their green shoots appear. Garlic and shallots are harvestable by the next summer.

- Remove cloves from bulb, but do not peel off papery skin.
- Plant the cloves flat side down, pointy side up, about 1-2 inches deep and 6-8 inches apart.
- Garlic and shallots need a full sun location with good drainage and soil free of weeds.

For more information on growing garlic and shallots, please see Chapter 10, A-Z Vegetables.

Fava beans

September and October are the time for planting fava beans by seed into raised beds or in-ground gardens. Fava beans need the overwintering process to develop an abundant spring harvest.

Overwintering vegetables

There are certain varieties of vegetables that are fall-planted for a spring harvest. These seed and vegetable starts are specifically marked as *overwintering varieties*. Some vegetables with overwintering varieties are broccoli, carrots, and leeks. Visit your local nursery for seeds and starts of overwintering vegetable varieties, and plant them in your raised bed or in-ground garden during September.

Autumn harvest

There is much to be harvested during the autumn in the Portland edible garden. Warm season summer veggies will become stunted and stop producing as the colder weather sets in; now is the time to harvest them in earnest for fresh eating and preservation. This includes: corn, cucumber, eggplant, peppers, pumpkins, summer squash, tomatoes, tomatillos, winter squash, and zucchini. This is also true for heat-loving summer annual herbs like basil.

Continue to harvest salad greens, lettuce, kale, chard, carrots, and beets as needed. In October and November, your summer-planted crops for a fall harvest should be ready. This autumn bounty includes Brussels sprouts, broccoli, cabbage, cauliflower, fennel, kale, kohlrabi, radish, rutabaga, parsnips, and turnips.

Harvesting tomatoes

The majority of the tomato harvest in the Portland edible garden is in August and September. Our summers are short and slow to start, not ideal tomato growing weather. I typically begin harvesting cherry tomatoes in July and really look forward to slicing and saucing varieties in August and September. I aim to have the tomato harvest completed by the beginning of October. Tomato plants suffer in the cooler night temperatures, and fruit is unlikely to ripen on the vine after September.

To encourage tomato plants to ripen their fruit quicker, you can completely stop watering in the end of August or beginning of September. September is a great time to heavily prune your tomato plants to force them into ripening the most viable fruit. Any stems with flowers or very small green fruit can be completely cut off. Leave on only the stems with the largest fruit.

> **To encourage tomato plants to ripen their fruit quicker, you can completely stop watering in the end of August or beginning of September.**

Leave tomato fruit on the plant to ripen unless night temperatures are dipping below 50 degrees or there is a heavy rain forecasted. When this is the case, I cut stems with large fruit and bring tomatoes with stem intact inside to ripen on the kitchen counter. Don't forget, those hard green tomatoes are excellent for using in recipes like chutney and fried green tomatoes.

This may seem like a lot of additional work. Tomatoes can be finicky growers in our Portland climate, and you will benefit from the little bit of extra effort.

Remember to always pull up your tomato plants and dropped fruit and remove from your garden. If it is not diseased, you can compost in your home compost maker. If disease and pests were problematic on your plant, or if your compost bin doesn't heat up high enough to kill seeds, then toss it all in your curbside yard debris bin.

Pumpkins and winter squash

These members of the squash family grow during the hot summer season and come to maturity in the early fall with a long storage life through winter. To ensure the longest winter storage, make sure the fruit's skin ripens to a hard shell by leaving it on the vine through autumn. In Portland gardens, the entire squash family is prone to a fungal disease called powdery mildew. The disease is soil-borne, spreads from leaf to leaf by overhead watering, and typically takes hold in the summer. Plants with powdery mildew look pretty ratty by September. Cut pumpkins and winter squash from the vine, dispose of infected vines in the trash or curbside yard debris bin, and let the fruit "harden off" laying in the garden.

Autumn gardening projects

In addition to harvesting, autumn is the perfect time for gardening projects. The temperatures have cooled, and I am eager to put some parts of the garden "to rest" for the winter. I look forward to cold and rainy winters spent indoors enjoying my contemplative activities like reading, writing, embroidery, art, yoga, and meditation. I appreciate the break after the hectic, busy spring, summer, and early fall.

Cleaning up the edible garden in fall is an essential part of garden health and productivity, along with crop rotation, companion planting, cover crops, and composting. Most diseases and pests are specific to vegetable plant families. Cleaning up and disposing properly of plant debris promotes a healthy garden with less pest and disease.

More information on plant families can be found in Chapter 3.

Around the beginning of October, I harvest the last of the spring/summer vegetables, herbs, and annual flowers from my raised bed garden. I leave in place my overwintering vegetables, like garlic, shallots, and leeks. If the plant debris is pest and disease free, I add it to my home compost maker. When disease and pests have been problematic, I toss this plant debris into the curbside yard debris bin or trashcan. Also, remember that if your home composting system doesn't heat up hot enough to kill seeds (mine doesn't!), then don't put seedy things in your compost maker. I have found this to be especially problematic with seeds from melon, cucumber, squash, pumpkin, and tomatoes. This also goes for annual flowers like cosmos, annual herbs like dill, and weeds. If you are attentive, a well-constructed compost pile can typically reach 130 degrees and quickly kill most seeds. However, some tenacious seeds need 30 days of 145 degrees to be killed off.[6]

---

6 http://wssa.net/2009/04/want-to-keep-your-compost-weed-free/

After cleaning up all spent plant material from your garden, you have a few options:

- **Just leave the garden bare until next spring**. Cool, it's easy! But bare soil also promotes weed growth, soil loss to erosion from rain, a playground for burrowing squirrels, and an ideal litter box for neighborhood cats.
- **Cover up your garden with cardboard, a tarp, or frost blanket** weighted or pinned down. This is straightforward and low cost, and doing so helps to prevent weed, erosion, squirrel, and cat problems!
- **Plant cover crops.** These fall-sown crops, like crimson clover, fava beans, oilseed radish, and so on, prevent weeds and erosion and benefit your soil life. They can be tilled under in spring and used as a "green manure." Win-win for your garden. The downside is that these seeds take a little bit to germinate and get growing, during which time the frantic fall-nut-burying squirrels could wreak havoc on your young seedbed. So keep an eye on it for intruders. Please see Chapter 4: Garden Care and Maintenance for full information on planting cover crops.
- **Sheet or lasagna mulch** your raised bed or in-ground garden. Fall is a perfect time for this fun and simple project that will build great garden soil for you by the next spring, when you are ready to start gardening again. You can even cover sheet mulching with a frost blanket or tarp, or plant cover crop seeds directly into the top layer. Please see Chapter 4: Garden Care and Maintenance for full information on sheet/lasagna mulching.

Along with planting cover crops, the sheet mulching technique in the fall will assist the gardener all winter long, preparing a happier, healthier garden come spring planting time.

September to-do list

- ❑ Harvest summer vegetable and herb crops.
- ❑ Plant cool season salad greens from seeds.
- ❑ Plant garlic and shallots from bulbs.
- ❑ Plant overwintering varieties of vegetables: fava beans, carrots, leeks, and broccoli.
- ❑ Apply organic slug bait every 2 weeks around vegetable crops and seed bed.
- ❑ After harvesting, clean up the garden by removing all plant material.
- ❑ Plant cover crops by seed.

❑ Utilize sheet mulching over raised or in-ground garden beds.

❑ Clean and store tomato cages, stakes, and trellises for winter.

❑ If your compost pile or bin is ready, you can spread compost on top of garden beds before covering for winter.

❑ Start a new compost pile or bin.

❑ Empty containers used to grow annual vegetables, herbs, and flowers. Clean with diluted bleach solution and rinse well. Store for next spring.

October to-do list

❑ Continue September to-do list.

❑ Harvest the last of the warm-season summer vegetable crops.

❑ Begin harvesting the cool-season vegetable crops planted for fall/winter harvest.

❑ Assess last year's frost blankets for damage and purchase new and additional ones as needed. Although my frost blankets get dirty and stained with annual use, I find they hold up for at least 5 years.

❑ If you are utilizing other season extension techniques like cold frames, low tunnels, or a greenhouse, prepare those now.

November to-do list

❑ Harvest cool season vegetable crops planted for fall/winter harvest.

❑ Continue to apply organic slug bait every 2 weeks as needed while slugs are still present. If frost temperatures arrive slugs become less active. Warmer winters equal more active slugs.

❑ Clean and store your garden tools for the winter, except for the leaf rake. I'm usually raking leaves until Christmastime.

❑ Build a leaf mulch pile with all of those fall leaves.

❑ Disconnect, drain, and store hoses. Cover outdoor spigots.

When November rolls around, I've usually harvested the last of the hardy cool season greens like kale. All I'm coming out to the garden for the remainder of the winter is fresh snips of herbs like parsley, cilantro, rosemary, and winter savory.

When the garden is put to rest for the winter, it's a perfect time to write a review of the year in your garden journal. What did you like? What didn't you like? What crops did well, and what crops were problematic? What were your favorite varieties, and what brought you the most joy? What required the most work? What would you never plant again, and what do you wish you had planted? Jot it all down because it will help you next year in planting your new garden.

Autumn shopping List

- Seeds for salad greens, overwintering carrot varieties, and fava beans
- Transplants for quick growing cool-season vegetables like lettuce, kale, and Swiss chard
- Transplants for overwintering vegetable varieties like leeks and broccoli
- Garlic and shallot bulbs
- Cover crop seeds
- Frost blankets
- Landscape pins (they look like large staples) to secure frost blankets and tarps
- Tarp or cardboard to cover garden beds
- Compost bin
- Organic slug bait
- Materials to build season extenders like cold frame and low tunnels

Notes

Notes

Notes

Section Three

10 / A-Z Guide to the Best Vegetables for Portland

This chapter is a compilation of my personal experience growing these vegetable crops. With the exception of asparagus, at one time or another, I have grown each of these vegetable crops in my own garden or a client's garden. I am happy to pass onto you my gardening experience, and my hope is these tips and tricks will help you become a more successful gardener.

For each vegetable profile, you will find my observations on culture, favorite varieties for our climate, planting, care, pests and disease, and harvesting information.

Each of these crops can be grown in your Portland area vegetable garden. Due to our climate and growing season, some will be more successful and abundant than others. The crops that can struggle with our climate and growing season are corn, eggplant, melons, and peppers.

Here are my top dozen easiest vegetables for beginner gardeners to start with:

Beans	Potatoes
Carrots	Radishes
Cucumbers	Scallions
Kale & Collards	Swiss Chard
Lettuce	Tomatoes
Peas	Zucchini

This chapter is not meant to be an exhaustive survey of all vegetables or of all vegetable gardening techniques. It is a jumping off point for new gardeners and food for thought for more experienced gardeners. And, if you are inspired to expand your vegetable crops, I am delighted!

ARTICHOKES and CARDOON

Cynara scolymus
C. cardunculus

Culture

Artichokes and cardoon originate in the Mediterranean, where for centuries they have been grown for cooking. The globe-shaped part of the artichoke we eat is an unopened flower bud. Cardoon, relatively unknown in American cooking, is grown for its thick fleshy stalks that have a mild artichoke-like flavor.

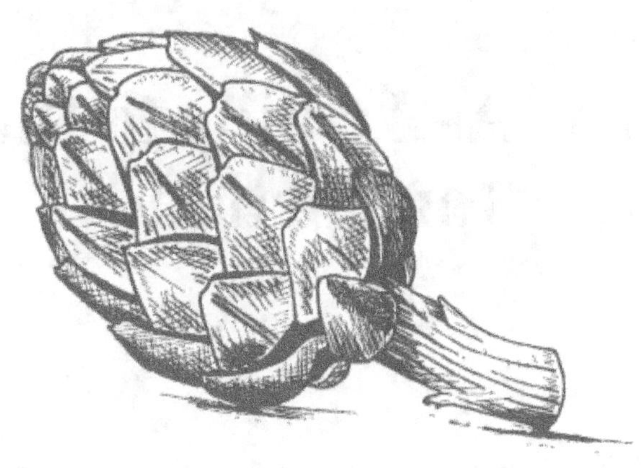

Artichokes and cardoon require a full sun location and rich, well-drained soil. They both become very large plants, 4 feet wide and 6 to 8 feet tall. Due to their size and perennial growth habit, both artichokes and cardoon require a lot of space in the edible garden. Their statuesque nature and lovely cascading serrated-edged, gray-green foliage make them interesting ornamental plants in the garden, so consider incorporating them outside of the dedicated edible garden.

Artichokes and cardoon are tender perennials that prefer cool summers and mild winters. In the maritime climate of the Portland metro area, artichoke plants typically will perennialize. Herbaceous perennials, artichoke and cardoon plants' foliage will die down during the winter. The crowns can die if soil temperature drops below 25 degrees.

Jolie's favorite varieties

Emerald, green globe, imperial star, and violetto grow well in Portland.

Planting artichokes and cardoon

If you prefer to start your own artichoke and cardoon plants from seeds, sow seeds indoors in January and February. Seedlings can be planted directly in the garden as early as April after all danger of frost has passed, but when the plants can still receive 10 to

12 days of temperatures below 50 degrees F. This is required to induce budding on artichokes. Seedlings can continue to be planted in the garden through May.

Select a garden site that receives full sun and is protected from wind and severe winter temperatures. Prepare the garden by amending with compost or manure and mixing in organic granular fertilizer. Plants prefer neutral pH soil for optimal production. If you are planting in native ground soil, which tends to be acidic, add garden lime prior to planting. Space plants at least 4 feet apart in all directions. I do not recommend growing artichokes in containers—in my experience the plants become too tall for container culture. Additionally, the plants are tender perennials, and when container plants are exposed to winter temperatures, they are more likely to die than those planted in ground.

Artichokes and cardoon care

Artichoke and cardoon are light-feeder plants and only require a once-a-year application of organic granular fertilizer each spring. Plants require consistent watering throughout the first growing season. However, soil should dry out between watering, as these plants prefer moist, not soggy, soil. In the second year, plants require consistent, thorough watering during the peak heat of summer. Once plants are three years old, they become quite drought tolerant.

In autumn before a hard frost, usually October and November, cut the plants to 8 to 10 inches above the soil, and mulch to keep the crowns from freezing over winter. Straw can be used for mulch; however, I prefer to mulch with autumn leaves or a shredded bark product.

All artichoke and cardoon plants have a limited life span and tend to lose their vigor, dying off within 3 to 5 years from planting. Replant new plants as needed.

Pests and disease

Aphids, crown rot, and powdery mildew can be problematic for these plants. In my experience, though, they are mostly-trouble free plants that thrive on neglect after established.

Harvesting artichokes and cardoon

Cardoon can be harvested at any time the stalks look thick and green. Cut stems completely off to the plant base when harvesting, and strip off leaves before cooking.

First-year artichokes will begin producing edible heads/buds in mid-summer, but several varieties will not produce artichokes the first year. The established plants are harvestable earlier in the late spring. Expect each plant to produce 3 to 6 artichokes each year.

Cut the heads/buds with 1 to 2 inches of stem attached. Harvest the heads/buds before the outer petals have begun to open. The smaller artichokes are the most tender and flavorful. If you do not harvest your artichokes before the petals open and they begin to bloom, rendering them inedible, leave the violet thistle-like flowers on the plant to attract and sustain bees.

ASIAN GREENS

Brassica spp.

Culture

Members of the broad *Brassica* family, this varied group of tasty leafy vegetables prevalent in Asian cooking includes mustard greens, choi, and Chinese cabbage. Though the individual varieties are diverse, they all thrive in the cool weather of spring and fall, with many remaining harvestable through the winter with minimal season extenders. Like other members of the Brassica family, the leafy greens, like mustards and choi, are typically easier to grow than the heading varieties, like Chinese cabbages. This group of plants tolerate a wide variety of soil conditions and can be grown in full or partial sun locations.

Jolie's favorite varieties

Chinese cabbage: China Express, Napa Blues, Scarlette
Mustards: Greenwave, Mizuna, Red Giant, Tah Tsai (spinach-type mustard)
Choi: Ching-Chiang, Violetta

Planting Asian greens

Chinese cabbage is most successful when planted by transplants into the garden during April. Mustards and choi can be planted successfully from seeds or starts. Plant starts directly in the garden during March and April, and seed directly in the garden when soil temperature has warmed up to 50 degrees, usually in April. Asian greens can all be planted again in August for an autumn and winter harvest. Space plants 12 inches apart.

Asian greens care

This group of plants are moderate feeders and benefit from application of organic granular fertilizer every 30 days throughout the growing season. Plants require consistent moderate watering throughout the growing season. Plants prefer cooler temperatures and are prone to premature bolting with temperature fluctuations, hot temperatures, and drought. Some of these factors can be prevented by following correct planting time and watering.

Pests and disease

Like other members of the *Brassica* family, aphids, cabbage moths, flea beetles, and slugs can bother these vegetables. Please see *Broccoli* and Chapter 4 for more information.

Harvesting Asian greens

Mustards and Choi are ready to harvest about 1 month from transplanting. Harvest the entire clump to 1 inch above the soil, and in another month a smaller clump will develop. Or like lettuce and other leafy greens, you can harvest outer leaves to maintain a continual harvest. Begin checking Chinese cabbages when their heads reach about 12 inches. You will know they are ready to harvest when the head is firm. Harvest entire cabbages by cutting the base of the plant off at soil level.

ASPARAGUS

Asparagus officinalis

Culture

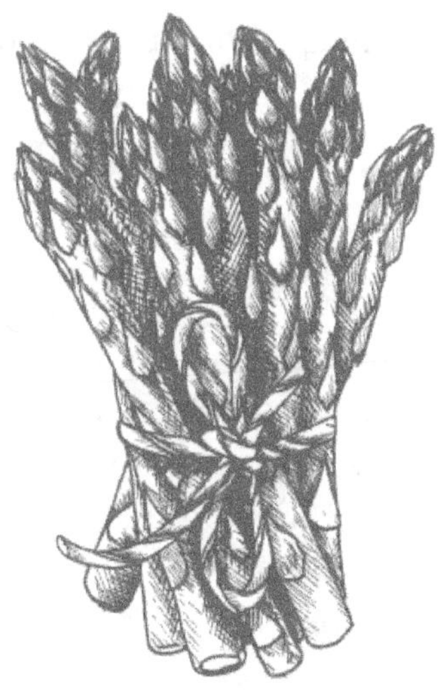

While writing and researching for this book, I realized asparagus is one of the few vegetable crops I have not actually grown. Asparagus, like artichoke, is a perennial vegetable in our Portland climate. A reliably hardy perennial, the tasty spears appear early in spring when there are few other fresh vegetables in the garden. Successfully growing asparagus requires an investment of time and space. After initial planting, expect 3 years until plants yield a full productive harvest. As a renter with small space gardens, I have not yet invested in growing asparagus. As a cook and foodie, I celebrate when the first locally grown asparagus arrives at the farmer's market and at my husband's produce department. It is a favorite of mine for spring dinners and brunch. I look forward to the day when I have a larger garden and can experiment with growing asparagus.

Jolie's favorite varieties

Asparagus varieties that grow well here and that can be found at local garden centers are Jersey Night, Mary Washington, Pacific Purple, and Sweet Purple.

Planting asparagus

Asparagus is grown from crowns (roots) that are stocked in local garden centers early in spring, around February into March. The crowns can be planted 4 to 6 weeks before average last frost. In Portland this is around March 1. Asparagus requires a full sun location with a garden bed rich in organic matter and free of weeds. Asparagus can be planted in raised beds or in-ground gardens. Containers are not recommended. The key to abundant production is loose soil full of compost.

Prepare your asparagus bed by digging a trench 12 inches wide and 6 inches deep. Rows should be spaced at least 3 feet apart. Add into the trench 1 to 2 cups of organic granular vegetable fertilizer per 10-foot row, and mix with 1 to 2 inches of compost. Now make a hill down the middle of the trench.

Prior to planting, soak asparagus crowns for 30 minutes in diluted liquid seaweed. After soaking, place the moistened crowns in the trench on the top of the hill with their roots draped over the sides. Crowns should be spaced 12 inches apart from each other without touching. Cover the crowns lightly with only 1 to 2 inches of soil. Initially, you only need just enough soil to cover the roots. As the asparagus grows, gradually fill in the trench at intervals so there are ultimately 6 to 8 inches of soil covering the crowns. Utilizing this gradual covering technique helps prevent the crowns from rotting in the cool, damp spring garden soil.

Asparagus care

In its first year, the asparagus bed needs consistent watering to remain evenly moist while the plants are establishing. Continue to irrigate regularly during the second year. By the third year, an asparagus bed is established and can be relatively drought tolerant.

Asparagus is a heavy-feeding crop and requires organic granular fertilizer every 30 days throughout the growing season. Additionally, garden lime can be applied to the soil surface every few years to keep the pH less acidic. Each year, spread about 2 inches of fresh compost over the top of the asparagus bed to ensure the crowns are below the soil surface.

To ensure health and best yields, keep the asparagus bed completely free of weeds. In the autumn, cut all yellow foliage and stalks completely to the ground and remove from the asparagus bed. This autumn cleaning-up technique will also promote a disease-free healthy asparagus bed.

Pests and disease

Asparagus beetles and slugs are the most common pests in the asparagus bed. Fungal diseases such as crown rot, fusarium wilt, and rust (needle blight) can trouble asparagus. Keeping the asparagus bed healthy by proper fertilizing, amending with compost, consistent watering, weeding, and autumn cleanup will help prevent disease from taking hold.

Harvesting asparagus

During the first year, allow asparagus plants to grow undisturbed with no harvest. In the second year, the spears can be lightly harvested for approximately 4 to 6 weeks until the subsequent shoots become very thin. By the third year, the asparagus patch will yield a full harvest season. Each successive year, the patch will increase in productivity and the harvest time will be a full 8 to 12 weeks.

To harvest asparagus spears, select when they are about 6 to 10 inches tall, and cut them off about 1 inch *below* the soil surface. Towards the end of the harvest season, leave the smaller spears to mature into ferns. This will regenerate the asparagus plants and keep the perennial bed growing year to year.

BEANS

Phaseolus vulgaris

Culture

I love growing beans in my garden. In my experience, they are super easy to grow and produce a lot! Beans, with the exception of favas, are a warm season crop planted in late spring and harvested throughout the summer. Bush, pole, and drying varieties of beans all need a full sun location, lightly moist soil, and minimal fertilizer. Pole beans grow into tall vines—some over 6 feet tall—and need to be supported with a strong trellis or tripod structure. They will yield a continuous harvest all summer. Bush beans grow to only around 2 feet tall and produce all at once.

I usually grow pole type beans on a trellis or tripod in my garden. This vertical gardening technique is an excellent use of the limited space in my small garden. Did you know that beans actually boost nitrogen in the soil? Additionally, they are not prone to many diseases or pests and therefore do not need to be rotated.

Jolie's favorite varieties

Violet-podded pole beans are super colorful surprises in the garden. Rattlesnake is an heirloom bean with speckled pods that can be eaten as a fresh edible-podded bean or left to mature and dry for winter cooking. Kentucky Wonder and Blue Lake Pole are both reliable standard green beans. Romano-type pole beans have a unique buttery taste; I like a yellow variety, Golden Gate. French/filet-type pole beans are slender and scrumptious. Consider also planting runner-type pole beans such as Scarlet Emperor with vibrant red flowers, and Sunset with peach blooms. Runner beans are very tall vines reaching up to 10 feet, they can be planted earlier than other beans (around April 15). They will grow in a partial sun location. Runner beans need at least 6 hours of sun a day for good flower and pod production. Their flowers are a hummingbird's delight, and the quick growing vines make a stunning ornamental screening plant.

Planting beans

All varieties of beans are best direct-seeded in the garden when the soil has warmed up to 60 degrees. Typically, in Portland, this is during May. Beans will not germinate or grow in cold soaked soil. Keep in mind these exceptions: runner beans can be planted earlier, around April 15, and fava beans are fall planted for overwintering and harvesting the following spring. Beans can also be planted from starts.

Bean care

Beans are not heavy feeders, and do not require fertilizer at planting time or during the growing season. Soil needs to be kept evenly moist while bean seeds are germinating. After germination, continue to provide consistent watering to keep the soil lightly moist.

Pests and disease

All types of beans can be prone to bean weevils, Mexican bean beetles, flea beetles, cucumber beetles, and spider mites. Diseases of the bean family include blights, rust, powdery mildew, mosaic virus, anthracnose, and root rot. However, in my experience, disease or pests do not typically trouble beans.

Harvesting beans

Once bean plants are producing, it is essential to check them daily and harvest. Snap beans and green beans are most tender and tasty when harvested at the size of a pencil. When pods become large, and you can see the outlines of bulging seeds, they tend to become very tough and stringy. Shelling beans are harvested when the seeds look large and fully formed but the pods are still green and soft. Drying beans are ready to harvest when pods have dried out, are stiff and easily broken open, but not shattered.

BEETS

Beta vulgaris

Culture

A member of the spinach family, beets are an annual cool-season vegetable crop grown for both their juicy earthy-tasting roots and delectable greens. Did you know beetroots come in not only red, but also gold, striped, and white? You can purchase beet seeds in mixes of colorful varieties! To develop good-sized roots, beets require a full sun location—however, they can also be grown for just greens in slightly less sun.

Jolie's favorite varieties

My favorite beets include Chioggia, an Italian heirloom beet that made its way to the U.S. in 1865. The Early Wonder Tall Top is adapted to all seasons, and the Detroit dark red is another heirloom beet, first seen in the U.S. in 1892. I also love Touchstone Gold beets, and Bull's Blood beets—the latter has gorgeous purple foliage.

Planting beets

Beets are best planted from seed directly into the garden. Over the last few years, I've seen beet transplants for sale, and I tried it one year as an experiment. I do not recommend planting beet transplants, as it is stressful and damaging to their long taproot. Beets perform best in evenly moist, loose, fertile soil with excellent drainage. Direct-seed beets in the garden when the soil temperature has warmed up to around 60 degrees. In Portland, this is typically in mid-April. Plant beets in April and May for a summer harvest and again in August through September for a late fall harvest. The seedbed should be kept evenly moist to ensure germination, but not overly soggy. Springs are unpredictable in Portland, and sudden temperature changes can cause beets to prematurely bolt.

Beets care

Beets are moderate feeders, and as they are growing, they appreciate regular application of organic fertilizer, particularly the nutrient phosphorus. Good organic sources of phosphorus are bone meal and rock phosphate. I like to use liquid seaweed, rich in trace minerals, for beets and other root vegetables because it is very helpful in encouraging root development. After germination, beets continue to need consistent watering and evenly moist soil.

Pests and disease

Leafminers, flea beetles, and aphids are the most common pests on beet leaves. Some diseases include powdery mildew, scab, and dampening off. In my experience, the entire spinach family—beets, spinach, Swiss chard—are extremely prone to leafminers.

Leafminers are tiny insects that burrow inside the leaf tissue. At first glance it looks like blackened, rotting leaves. Leafminers attack the beet greens, not the roots. To prevent leafminers, it is imperative to rotate the entire spinach family on a 2- to 4-year rotation. When I see the beginning of leafminers, I remove and destroy all the leaves with leafminer trails. See Chapter 4 for detailed information on leafminers.

You can spray leaves with organic products like horticultural oil, neem oil, and spinosad. Keep in mind, horticultural oil is highly toxic to bees. Neem has a lower toxicity to bees. Spinosad is highly toxic to both butterfly larvae and bees. Horticultural oil and neem oil have a lower toxicity if they are sprayed at night when bees are not active.

Harvesting beets

Beets can begin being harvested for baby roots about 4 to 5 weeks after planting seeds. Beets are most tender when smaller, around 2 to 3 inches in diameter. Large beets left in the ground too long can become woody and tough.

Harvest beet greens as needed. Remember, if you harvest too many greens, the roots will suffer in development. Harvest 1 or 2 leaves from each plant to keep everything healthy.

BROCCOLI

Brassica oleracea

Culture

I love broccoli so much that I eat it daily year-round. Broccoli is an annual cool-season vegetable from Italy that thrives in full sun and rich, well-fertilized soil. It is a member of the *Brassica* family, along with cauliflower and cabbage.

The typical broccoli crown we eat is the plant's unopened flower buds. Sprouting broccoli varieties form smaller heads and side shoots rather than one large crown. Broccolini—or Baby Broccoli—is a hybrid cross between broccoli and Chinese kale. It has smaller broccoli flowerets on long, tender stalks. Broccoli Raab, sometimes called Rapini, is not a true broccoli and is actually more closely related to a turnip. Raab/rapini never forms a crown and instead is harvested for its tender stems, leaves, and small, unopened flower buds. In 2018, I discovered an Italian heirloom, "Leaf Broccoli," grown solely for its delicious leaves. I found it to have a delicious taste, with leaves of a soft texture somewhere between kale and collards.

Jolie's favorite varieties

My favorite broccoli includes Apollo, which has long stemmed side shoots. I also love Summer Purple, Umpqua (a late-season broccoli), and DiCicco, an Italian heirloom with side shoots that was introduced to the U.S. in 1890. Spigariello Liscia—a leaf broccoli—and Romanesco, a fractal-shaped veggie that resembles a mix of broccoli and cauliflower, are other favorites.

Planting broccoli

I recommend planting broccoli from transplants rather than direct seeding in the garden. Plant broccoli transplants in the garden March through May. Depending on variety, broccoli is typically ready for harvest 60-80 days from transplanting. Broccoli transplants can be planted again in July and August for a fall harvest. Plant overwintering varieties in September for a late winter/early spring harvest.

Broccoli care

Broccoli prefers evenly moist soil and is a heavy feeder. Apply an organic vegetable fertilizer at planting time and regular intervals throughout the growing season. Broccoli is a cool-season vegetable that thrives in the cooler temperatures of spring and fall. Inconsistent temperature fluctuations can cause broccoli to quickly bolt: the crowns and side shoots will open to yellow flowers.

The good news is that these flowers are edible and taste slightly mustardy, so don't let them go to waste! In extreme heat, broccoli can also develop tough bitter crowns. Monitor temperatures, and if sudden hotter temperatures are projected, you can harvest the crowns. Or, if left in the ground, you can water them well and cover them with a shade cloth to help prevent premature bolting.

Pests and disease

In my experience, broccoli is mostly disease free. However, pests can be a major problem. Aphids, cabbage moths, and flea beetles prey on broccoli. To maintain good soil health and prevent disease and pests, it is imperative to rotate all *Brassica* family crops on a 4-year rotation.

Aphids and cabbage moths love all members of the *Brassica* family. Aphids can be dealt with by daily monitoring and hosing off plants. Aphid populations decline later in the season, so sometimes broccoli planted for a fall harvest is less troubled by aphids. If you need to spray for aphids, a less toxic organic approach is Neem oil, applied at night.

Cabbage moths are actually butterflies, and they are active during the day. Around April, you will begin spotting the small white butterfly flying in a "drunkenly" pattern throughout the garden looking for host plants. She lays her eggs on *Brassica* family plants for her hungry larvae to munch on. Cabbage moth caterpillars are camouflaged green, and usually reside on the underside of leaves. New caterpillars are tiny, only the size of a fingernail's thickness. As the hungry caterpillars munch on *Brassica* plants, skeletonizing the leaves, they grow quite large and fat. The best approach for dealing with cabbage moths is to provide a barrier to prevent eggs from being laid. This is also a successful strategy for preventing aphids. Cover the entire bed with a floating row cover, or coat leaves with kaolin clay. This will have the least impact on other butterflies, bees, and beneficial bugs. Organic sprays to target cabbage moth caterpillars are Bt and spinosad. Keep in mind that if you spray for the pest cabbage moth, you are also inadvertently spraying for beneficial butterflies you may be trying to attract to your garden.

Harvesting broccoli

Harvest standard broccoli when the main crown reaches anywhere from 1-6 inches across. Crowns should be tight, dense, and green. Heads that are loose, yellowing, or bolted into flowers are past their prime. Cutting the main head when it is at a smaller size will encourage greater growth of side shoots. Regular cutting of side shoots will encourage continued production. Sprouting broccoli is usually ready to harvest around 60 days from transplant. Harvest florets continuously over several months.

BRUSSELS SPROUTS

Brassica oleracea

Culture

The much maligned and hated Brussels sprout of my childhood was purchased frozen in a plastic bag and boiled to death into a mushy brown mess. As an adult, I rediscovered Brussels sprouts by lightly sautéing them in olive oil and eating them slightly browned on the edges, bright green, and the perfect texture, somewhere between soft and crunchy. My husband—who was never been big on vegetable experimentation—was won over when I cooked Brussels sprouts with bacon, dried cranberries, pine nuts, and fresh rosemary.

Growing Brussels sprouts can sometimes be a challenge for the urban gardener. Brussels sprouts perform best in cool weather but are slow growing over a long season. The key to their success is proper timing. These large, tall plants are heavy feeders and require moist rich soil. Most Brussels sprouts are green; however, Rubine is a sweet-looking heirloom variety with purple-red sprouts.

Jolie's favorite varieties

My favorite Brussels sprouts include the heirloom purple Rubine, and Long Island Improved.

Planting Brussels sprouts

I recommend planting Brussels sprouts from transplants. Several years in a row I tried planting Brussels sprouts in June and July for a fall harvest. I never saw good production for a fall harvest before frosts set in. I have seen Brussels sprouts planting recommended in April or May for a summer harvest. But why would you want to eat Brussels sprouts in the summer when gardens are bursting with tomatoes, cucumbers, and beans? Brussels sprouts are the quintessential fall and winter vegetable that I think tastes better after a few frosts have nipped the plants. After several years of unsuccessful attempts to grow

Brussels sprouts, a farmer friend gave me an excellent tip. She advised I plant Brussels sprout transplants in the garden as early as April for a fall harvest. In her experience, it really did take the slow growing Brussels sprouts that long to mature.

Caring for Brussels sprouts

Brussels sprouts appreciate regular watering and evenly moist soil. They are heavy feeders and require an organic vegetable fertilizer at planting time and at regular intervals while growing.

Pests and disease

Like other members of the *Brassica* family, aphids, cabbage moths, flea beetles, and occasionally powdery mildew prey on Brussels sprouts. Please see *Broccoli* for more information, as well as Chapter 4.

Harvesting Brussels sprouts

Harvest buds when they are 1-2 inches, tight, and well formed. Pick Brussels sprouts from the bottom of the plant. The upper buds will continue to mature after the lower are harvested.

CABBAGE

Brassica oleracea

Culture

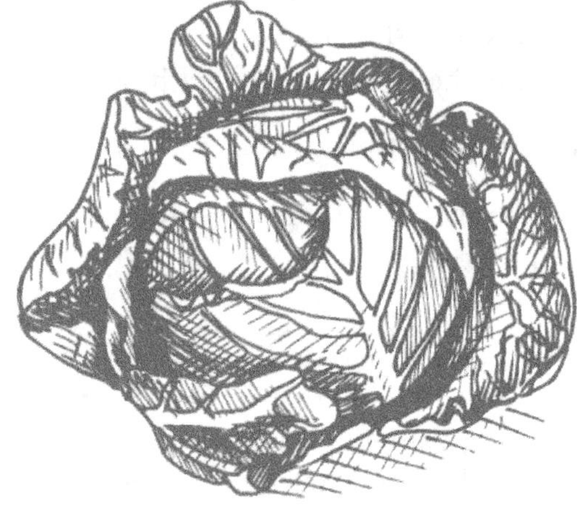

Cabbage is a member of the large *Brassica* family and is a reliable crop with varieties for every season. This makes it a year-round harvest vegetable. With leaves in the full spectrum from purple, blue, green, yellow, to white, and with both crinkled savoy type leaves and smooth leaves, cabbage is a striking ornamental plant. Its versatility in cooking make cabbage an indispensable home-grown vegetable, if you have the space. Each plant averages 2 feet around, so don't crowd them. Cabbage requires a full sun location and thrives in rich well-draining soil. Plants can be temperamental to sudden temperature changes that will cause heads to split open.

Jolie's favorite varieties:

Charmant, Early Jersey Wakefield, January King, Kalibos, Late Flat Dutch, Ruby Ball, Tiara, and Tundra.

Planting cabbage

Select a full sun location and amend soil with compost and organic granular fertilizer. For best success, plant cabbage directly into the garden with seedlings. Seedlings can be planted into the garden around April 1st. Space plants 2 feet apart from each other.

For a spring and summer harvest, plant April to June with spring/summer varieties with 45-90 days to maturity. For a fall and winter harvest, plant June to August with fall/winter varieties with 60-90 days to maturity. For a harvest the following spring, plant overwintering varieties with 180 to 200 days to maturity in August.

Cabbage care

Cabbage is a moderate feeder and requires application of organic granular fertilizer every 30 days throughout the growing season. However, do not over fertilize, as cabbage plants exposed to high applications of fertilizer may result in poor head shape and reduced yields. Cabbage need consistent watering and evenly moist soil.

Pest and disease

Like other members of the Brassica family, cabbage is prone to aphids, cabbage moths, flea beetles, and slugs. See *Broccoli* and Chapter 4 for more information.

Harvesting cabbage

Early varieties of cabbage mature fast and can burst quickly if not harvested promptly. Harvest these as soon as the heads are well formed and at mature size. Later maturing varieties of cabbage hold in the garden much longer. Fall varieties can be kept in the garden for several months without head splitting. To harvest, cut heads from the stems at ground level, including 3 outer leaves to protect against bruising.

CARROTS

Daucus carota var. sativus

Culture

Carrots are grown for their sweet, crispy roots. Every week, I cook a big batch of nutritious creamy carrot soup to eat for my breakfast. Carrots can be planted spring and summer in a full-sun location with light, loose, fine textured soil. There are many varieties of carrots, and you can even grow short, round varieties, like Parisienne or Rondo, in a container! We are accustomed to seeing only orange carrots—did you know that carrots come in white, yellow, orange, red, and purple? Wouldn't it be fun to plant some colorful varieties in your garden? I like to buy a rainbow seed mix.

Jolie's favorite varieties

You already know I love the rainbow seed mix, a combination of white, yellow, coral, salmon, and orange carrots. Dragon carrots are purple on the outside and orange on the inside. Paris Market are round, orange 19th century heirloom carrots, and Scarlet Nantes are orange 1850's French heirlooms. Yaya are an orange, early carrot; Nutri-Red is a salmon-red carrot; and Yellowstone is—you guessed it—a lemon yellow carrot.

Planting carrots

I recommend planting carrots directly in the garden from seeds. Plant seeds when the soil has warmed up to around 60 degrees. In my experience, this is usually in mid-April. Carrot seeds will not germinate in cold, soaked soil. For a continuous harvest summer into fall, successively plant carrot seeds every 2 to 3 weeks through July. Carrots need well-worked loose soil to grow well-formed roots. Heavy clay soil and rocks will result in forked roots. Carrot seeds are slow to germinate and can take up to 20 days, so be patient. The seedbed must be kept evenly moist to prevent the soil from crusting and preventing good germination. On warm sunny days, I sometimes need to lightly mist the carrot seedbed twice a day.

Dig a row 1/4 to 1/2 inch deep, sow carrot seeds, and then cover with a light layer of peat moss, vermiculite, or sand. Covering the seedbed with a piece of row cover or burlap can keep soil warm and moist during germination. For several years, I had so much trouble growing carrots. In hindsight, I realized I was planting the seeds too deeply, there was too much woody compost covering the seed bed, and I wasn't patient enough to wait 3 to 4 weeks for the seeds to germinate.

Carrot care

Carrots are light feeders and do not require supplemental fertilizing. Typically, I am only fertilizing the raised bed when I prepare it for planting. Once seeds have germinated, carrots need consistent watering and evenly moist soil. Over fertilizing can cause hairy roots and overwatering can cause cracked roots. When plants are 4 inches tall, begin thinning them to 1 to 3 inches apart. When carrot plants have about 7 to 10 leaves, hill 1 to 2 inches of soil around the tops to prevent green shoulders.

Pests and disease

Carrot fly maggots, slugs, blight, mildews, and damping off can trouble carrots. In my experience, carrots are usually pest and disease free. Trouble typically manifests as lack of proper germination due to moisture and temperature fluctuations.

Harvesting carrots

Most carrot varieties are best harvested for the sweetest flavor around 3/4 inch to 1 inch in diameter. Watering your carrot bed before harvest will assist carrots in absorbing maximum water capacity and loosening the soil. Harvest carrots by gently pulling their green leafy tops. If the tops break off, loosen the soil around carrots. Remove carrot tops from roots before storing in the refrigerator, as the green tops will pull moisture from the roots and cause limp carrots.

Compost your carrot tops or feed them to your chickens and rabbits. My friend Freya the rabbit loves to eat carrot tops! Carrot tops are edible for humans, too, and if you are daring, experiment with sautéing them or making a pesto from them.

CAULIFLOWER

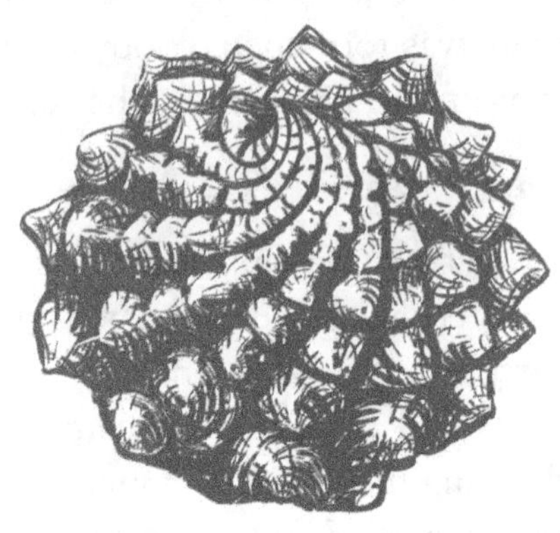

Brassica oleracea

Culture

Cauliflower is another member of the vast *Brassica* family, and it is most closely related to broccoli, Brussels sprouts, cabbage, and kale. Of the five crops, in my experience, cauliflower is tied for the most challenging to grow along with Brussels sprouts. But do not be discouraged! I have grown lovely and tasty cauliflower plants in several spring seasons. Cauliflower is a cool season vegetable best planted in spring and again in late summer through early fall. It is very sensitive to high temperatures.

The name cauliflower means "cabbage flower" coming from the Italian word *cavolfiore*, with origins from Latin *caulis* (stalk) and *floris* (flower). Cauliflower is a cool season vegetable crop best planted in spring and autumn. Cauliflower requires a full sun location in rich well-drained soil with a neutral pH. We are most familiar with common white cauliflower; however, cauliflower varieties also include yellow, purple, and green.

There seem to be lots of differing opinions if the Romanesco variety is a cauliflower, a broccoli, or a cross of both. No matter its vegetable classification, Romanesco is exquisite, bearing unique clusters of swirling chartreuse spires. Further increasing the fascination with this spectacular variety is the fact that the number of spirals on its head are a Fibonacci number.

Jolie's favorite varieties

Cheddar, Purple of Sicily, Romanesco, Snowball

Planting cauliflower

Select a full sun location and amend soil with compost and organic granular fertilizer. In my experience, cauliflower is more successful when planted in the garden from seedlings versus seeds. If you want to start your own plants from seeds, sow seeds indoors in February. Plant seedlings in the garden beginning April 1st. Plants should be 2 feet apart. Plant cauliflower through April until the beginning of June. Cauliflower can be planted again in the end of August for a fall-into-winter harvest.

Care for cauliflower

Cauliflower is a heavy feeder and requires monthly applications of organic granular fertilizer throughout the growing season. However, high levels of nitrogen can cause leaves to grow through the heads, so do not over fertilize. Cauliflower plants require consistent water and evenly moist soil. Stress from drought, inconsistent watering, temperature fluctuations, and high temperatures can all cause plants to bolt and develop uneven open heads.

Pests and disease

Like other Brassica family plants, cauliflower is prone to aphids, cabbage moths, flea beetles, and slugs. See *Broccoli* and Chapter 4 for more information.

Harvesting cauliflower

In my experience, homegrown cauliflower does not reach the large size of grocery store purchased cauliflower. It is more of a baseball to softball size versus a football size. Please keep that in mind when you are determining if your cauliflower plants are at harvestable maturity. When cauliflower florets/heads have reached their days to maturity, are at their maximum size, and are tight and dense, they are ready to harvest. Overly mature heads/florets past their prime begin to separate and appear "ricey." To harvest, cut the entire head with some leaves attached from the main stem.

If you would like to blanch your cauliflower to produce pure white heads, this must be done before harvesting. To blanch, when the cauliflower head is the size of a baseball (usually a few weeks before harvest), bunch some leaves loosely over the head, and secure them with twine.

CELERY and CELERIAC

Apium graveolens var. dulce
A. graveolens var. rapaceum

Culture

Celery is grown for the stems, leaves, and seeds. Celeriac, also called celery root, is grown for its baseball-sized swollen root. Both types of celery are water hogs and require fertile, well-draining soil. Celery is an annual vegetable that prefers a long warm growing season, and mature plants can tolerate mild winter temperatures.

Jolie's favorite varieties

The celery and celeriac you'll find in my garden include Red Adventure red celery; Pink Plume purple heirloom celery; Tango early maturing green celery; and Mars or Brilliant celeriac.

Planting celery

Plant celery from starts after risk of frost has passed, when night temperatures are consistently above 55 degrees and soil temperature is 60-65 degrees. Celery plants will bolt if exposed to prolonged night temperatures below 55 degrees. The timing of celery planting is the same as tomatoes. In Portland, night temperatures are usually consistently above 55 degrees in May and June.

Plant celeriac from seeds or starts in April or May for a summer harvest, and in June or July for a fall/winter harvest.

Celery care

Celery and celeriac are heavy feeders. They require organic vegetable fertilizer at planting time and regular intervals throughout the growing season. These plants love water and need more watering than most plants in the vegetable garden. Inconsistent watering that allows plants to dry out will cause dry, tough stalks.

I think this is why I experienced problems growing both celery and celeriac in different years: they were planted in mixed raised beds and did not receive the soaking watering they required. Prevent this by planting celery and celeriac exclusively, or combine with other water loving vegetables like lettuce, cucumbers, and melon.

Pests and disease

Celery is a member of the carrot family and can be bothered by carrot fly, as well as aphids, flea beetles, and blights. In my experience, with correct planting timing, ample water, regular fertilization, and crop rotation, celery is mostly pest and disease free.

Harvesting celery

Celery and celeriac have a long growing season to maturity at around 100 days. Harvest celery stalks as needed for a continual harvest throughout the summer and fall. Entire celery bunches can be harvested, but it is best to leave the plant in the garden until needed for cooking. Many celery varieties will last in the winter garden for continual harvesting if temperatures are above 20 degrees. Celeriac roots are ready to be harvested after a fall frost by digging up the entire root. Like many fall harvested veggies, a nip of frost will improve their sweet flavor.

CORN

Zea mays

Culture

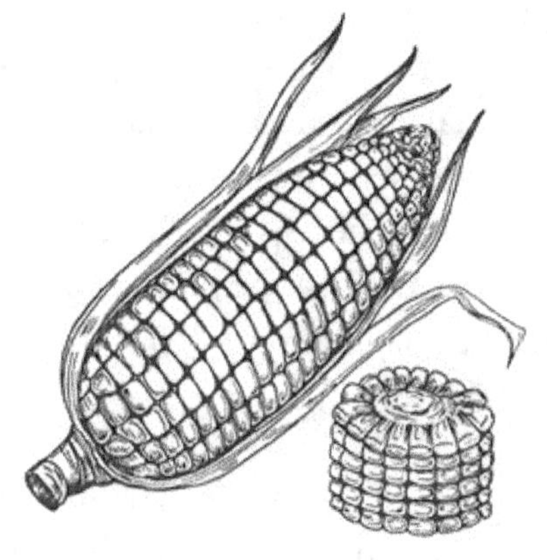

Corn is a member of the extensive grass family *Poaceae* (formerly *Gramineae*) that includes other edible crops: barley, millet, oats, rice, rye, spelt, sugarcane, and wheat. Agricultural grasses are grown for their edible seeds, called cereals or grains. Worldwide, corn is one of the top three grain crops grown. Types of corn include sweet corn for fresh eating, popcorn, flour corn, and ornamental corn. Corn is also called Maize and was cultivated by Indigenous people of Mexico over 10,000 years ago before spreading as a staple food crop throughout South, Central, and North America.

Corn is a warm season vegetable crop that requires full sun, hot temperatures, fertile soil, and lots of water. Most varieties will produce 1 to 2 ears per plant. Corn plants are wind pollinated, so for proper pollination to occur, individual varieties must be planted in blocks of at least 4 rows. Growing in our Portland climate, and especially in small space urban gardens, can be challenging. The key to a successful homegrown harvest is waiting until temperatures are optimal, planting a large enough corn patch for wind pollination, and keeping varieties separated by at least 200 feet to reduce cross pollination.

153

Jolie's favorite varieties

Bodacious, Golden Bantam, Golden Jubilee, Honey & Cream, Silver Queen, and Sugar Buns.

Planting corn

Select a full sun location and amend the soil well with compost and organic matter. Corn is a heavy feeder and requires high nitrogen during the vegetative stage. Apply a high nitrogen organic granular fertilizer to the soil before planting. Corn prefers a neutral pH, so apply lime if you are planting in native ground soil.

As corn thrives in hot weather, it is imperative to not plant too early. Like other warm season vegetable crops, corn requires night temperatures consistently above 55 degrees, so it is best planted mid-May through mid-June. For proper wind pollination, corn needs to be planted in blocks of at least 4 rows with at least 4 plants per row. Unless you have a large garden space, only plant one variety of corn. If you would like to plant multiple varieties of corn, space the varieties at least 200 feet apart to discourage cross pollination.

Corn is optimally planted by seeds directly in the garden when soil temperatures have warmed up to at least 65 degrees F. Seeds should be planted 1 to 2 inches deep and spaced 4 inches apart. Once they germinate, plants should be thinned to 12 inches apart.

Corn can also be planted by seedlings, but corn roots dislike disturbance, so be careful when transplanting.

Corn care

Corn is a heavy feeder. Apply organic granular fertilizer high in nitrogen at planting time and once a month throughout the season. You can also supplement with fish emulsion every 7-14 days until the plants develop tassels. Corn can be a drought tolerant plant, but to ensure optimum growth and maximum yield, keep it watered evenly and deeply. This is especially important during the tasseling stage of growth.

Pests and disease

Common insects on corn are corn borer and corn ear worm. Damping-off occurs in cool wet weather, preventing seedlings from emerging and causing seedlings to die off. Planting corn when the weather has warmed up enough, usually June here in Portland, can prevent this. Fungal diseases, including corn smut, blight, and rust, can occur. It is important to rotate corn in the vegetable garden. In the three years I grew corn, I had no pest or disease issues; my problem was getting plants to develop ears.

Harvesting corn

Sweet corn varieties are harvestable approximately 3 weeks from when the first silks appear on the baby ears. Drying and browning of the silks is also a sign of harvestable maturity. Harvest ears when the kernels are full and milky. For best flavor, corn should be refrigerated immediately after harvest, where it will hold its flavor for 2-4 days. Sweet corn is best eaten right after harvesting.

Popcorn, flour corn, and ornamental corn varieties are harvested when the husks turn brown and are partially dried. Hang corn ears in a well-ventilated, dry, warm area until they are fully dried. Popcorn kernels are ready for storage when they easily rub off the cob.

CUCUMBER

Cucumis sativus

Culture

Cucumbers are a tasty, succulent member of the large cucurbits family that also includes squash and melons. An annual warm season vegetable that requires a full sun location, cucumbers are planted in May and June when soil and air temperatures have significantly risen. Cucumbers typically are vines that will climb trellises, and there are also compact bush varieties for containers and smaller gardens. This summer vegetable thrives in hot temperatures, with regular watering and fertilizing and rich, well-drained soil. Cucumbers are ready to continually harvest by mid-summer and into the fall before frost. Grow different varieties for slicing and pickling.

Jolie's favorite varieties

I am especially fond of heirloom Lemon cucumbers for their tennis ball size, round shape, yellow color, and citrusy flavor. I also like the traditional Chinese variety, Suyo Long; the white Boothby's Blonde; and Marketmore for its disease resistance. Homemade Pickle cucumbers are disease resistant and are a great pickler. Last but not least, I am a fan of Patio Snacker cucumbers because they are compact and good in containers.

Planting cucumbers

Cucumbers are planted when soil temperatures have risen to 60 degrees and night temperatures are consistently above 55 degrees. In Portland, this is anywhere from mid-May into late June. Cucumbers will not tolerate any frost and are prone to rotting out in cold, wet soil. Plant cucumbers from starts or direct seeding in the garden. Given warm temperatures, cucumber seeds are quick to germinate, 1 to 2 weeks. I typically plant cucumbers next to an A-frame or trellis. Vertical gardening is a space saver in my small-space garden.

Cucumber care

Cucumbers are heavy feeders and require organic vegetable fertilizer at planting time and at regular intervals throughout the growing season. These plants, composed of 90 percent water, will perform best with consistent ample watering. Water stress causes poor fruit growth and fruits to have misshapen skinny parts and a bitter taste.

Pests and disease

Cucumber beetles and melon aphids can bother cucumbers, though in my experience cucumbers are mostly pest free. A variety of fungal problems plague cucumbers and other members of the cucurbits family, including powdery mildew, cucumber mosaic virus, and wilt. 4-year crop rotation will assist in preventing fungal problems.

Most fungal diseases are soil borne, so overhead watering will spread disease. Using a watering wand, drip irrigation, or soaker hoses will help prevent fungal diseases. Applying compost tea as a foliar spray and soil drench on a 2- to 3-week interval can be very successful in preventing and combatting powdery mildew. Pollination is critical for cucumbers as they bear male and female flowers on the same plant. A pollinator must visit both flowers for pollination and fruit set to occur. Attract pollinators by companion-planting flowers. You'll find more on powdery mildew in Chapter 4.

Harvesting cucumbers

Cucumbers provide a continual harvest throughout summer and into fall. Consistent picking, sometimes daily, of cucumbers will keep the plant productive. Harvest fruits when the flowers have fallen off and they have reached the appropriate size for their variety. Cucumber plants will not tolerate a frost, so complete the harvest by September. Harvest for pickling when cucumbers are 1.5 to 5 inches long.

EGGPLANT

Solanum melongena

Culture

Eggplant is a striking member of the *Solanaceae* family, along with potatoes, peppers, and tomatoes. The *Solanaceae* family is also called the "nightshade family" or "deadly nightshades" because all other parts of the plants—stems, leaves, and berries—are poisonous. Eggplant is a staple vegetable in European, Middle Eastern, and Asian cooking. Many people are only acquainted with the oblong dark purple varieties, though eggplant also comes in shades of white, pink, lavender, green, orange, and bi-colors.

Eggplant requires a long hot growing season to set fruit. They are extremely sensitive to cool temperatures below 55 degrees F. Optimum growth occurs with day temperatures of 80-90 degrees F and night temperatures above 70 degrees F. For these reasons, it can be challenging for eggplant to yield a good harvest in Portland. Select varieties with days to maturity in the 45-75 day range. There are even container varieties available, like Fairy Tale (65 days to maturity), Ophelia (55 days to maturity), and Patio Baby (45 days to maturity). These compact, quicker-maturing varieties are excellent solutions for small space gardens and our cool, short Portland summers.

Jolie's favorite varieties

In addition to the ones mentioned above, my favorites are Gretel, Hansel, Little Finger, and Orient Express.

Planting eggplant

Select a full sun location with fertile soil well-amended with compost and organic matter. Eggplant is a heavy feeder, so mix in organic granular fertilizer prior to planting. Place in each planting hole a tablespoon each of lime and bonemeal or rock phosphate to prevent blossom end rot.

Eggplant is a heat-loving plant that requires a long growing season to produce fruit, so it is always planted from seedlings, not seeds, in the garden. Space plants 18 inches apart.

Plant seedlings when the night temperatures are consistently above 55 degrees F. This typically means between May 15 through June 15. Plants are stunted when exposed to temperatures below 55 degrees. Utilizing a black or silver plastic mulch below plants,

157

and a cold frame or cloche around plants, can help increase temperatures at planting time until summer temperatures arrive in July.

Eggplant care

Eggplant is a heavy feeder and benefits from organic granular fertilizer applied at 30-day intervals throughout the growing season. Plants will yield more fruit if they are consistently deeply watered throughout the growing season. Eggplants can become heavy with fruit, so staking them for support can prevent stems from breaking.

Pests and disease

Blight, blossom end rot, flea beetles, and potato beetles can be a problem for eggplant. Practice a 4-year crop rotation of all *Solanaceae* family plants. See Chapters 3 and 4 for more information.

Harvesting eggplant

Eggplants are ready to harvest at their days to maturity, when fruit has reached mature size, fruit is firm, and when the skin is shiny and smooth. Eggplants past their prime will be soft, and the seeds inside will begin to darken. Cut individual eggplants off stems with sharp pruners or a garden knife, being careful of thorns on the plants.

FENNEL

Foeniculum vulgare

Culture

Florence fennel, also called bulb fennel or finocchio, is a type of fennel grown for its swollen stem base and eaten as a vegetable. The delicate fronds are also a tasty flavoring in cooking. Fennel is a cool season annual vegetable grown in the spring and fall. It grows happily in full sun, or in slightly less sun, 6 to 8 hours per day. Fortunately, Florence fennel is not a rampant spreader like the herb Bronze fennel (*Foeniculum vulgare*), which is considered an invasive species in Oregon.

Jolie's favorite varieties

Perfection is the standard fennel; it's a superior selection for our maritime northwest climate.

Planting fennel

Fennel can be planted from starts or by direct seeding in the garden. Plant fennel seeds or starts in the early spring, March to April, for a harvest in about 75-80 days. For a fall harvest, plant fennel again in August through September.

Fennel care

Fennel is a light feeder and does not require supplemental fertilizing. I usually only apply liquid seaweed at planting time. Fennel needs consistent water throughout the growing season.

Pests and disease

In my experience, fennel is disease and pest free.

Harvesting fennel

Fennel is ready to harvest in about 75-80 days. Fluctuations in temperature can cause fennel to develop a hard woody center. Harvest "bulbs" on the smaller side if temperatures are forecasted to spike above 80 degrees.

GARLIC

Allium sativum

Culture

Garlic is a spicy member of the allium family grown for its papery multi-clove bulbs. In Portland, garlic does best when fall-planted and harvested the next summer. Garlic requires a full sun location with fertile, well-drained soil.

There are two classes of garlic: softneck and hardneck. Softneck garlic tends to have a milder flavor and a longer storage life. These plants produce cloves in several layers around a soft central stem that is excellent for braiding. Hardneck varieties have a diverse range of strong flavors. Their cloves are easier to peel, and they have a shorter storage life than softneck garlic. Hardneck garlic cloves grow in a single circle around a central woody stem. In the spring, this woody stem produces a beautiful

159

tall flower stalk called a "scape" that is a gourmet culinary treat. Elephant garlic is not a true garlic, related more closely to a leek.

Jolie's favorite varieties

My favorite garlics include hardnecks Spanish Roja, Mount Hood, and Music. For softnecks, I prefer Early Red Italian and Inchelium Red.

Planting garlic

In Portland, we fall-plant garlic in September through the end of October. Plant garlic from bulbs obtained at a nursery. There are a wide range of varieties with different skin colors and flavor profiles. I like to grow one variety each of hardneck and softneck. Choose a full sun location and prepare the fall garden soil with compost and organic vegetable fertilizer. Separate each clove from the bulb and do not peel off the papery skin. Plant each clove root side down (pointed tip up) about 1 to 2 inches deep and 4 to 6 inches apart. If you miss the fall planting window, you have a second opportunity. Though not ideal, you can plant garlic in the spring. Expect spring-planted garlic to mature later than fall planted, for a harvest in the early fall. In the spring, you can find garlic as bulbs or potted starts.

Garlic care

In the fall, water garlic until the rainy season starts. In the spring, begin supplemental watering when it is not raining. Garlic likes moist soil while it is growing leafy greens. Provide organic vegetable fertilizer through the growing season. By early summer, garlic is not producing new leaves and is concentrating on forming bulbs. When bulb development begins, stop fertilizing and decrease watering. When hardneck varieties develop their flowering stalks, cut these stalks off when they are 6 inches tall to ensure energy is redirected to bulb development. These beautiful, delicious scapes can be used raw or cooked like green onions.

Pests and disease

Garlic is mostly disease and pest free. I have, however, had problems with black aphids on all my allium family crops. I totally thought garlic was pest free and actually deters pests from the garden due to its strong smell, so I was surprised to find hundreds of tiny black aphids sucking the life out of the tender new growth. During the fall into winter, when beneficial bugs are not so active, I would spray aphids on garlic with organic neem oil or insecticidal soap. In the active growing season, aim to attract ladybugs to prey on the pesky aphids. I have also seen fungal diseases on garlic in a friend's garden. Fungal diseases can be prevented by a 4-year crop rotation, good garden hygiene and clean up, and foliar spraying compost tea.

Harvesting garlic

Fall-planted garlic is usually ready to begin harvesting around July, depending on the variety. Garlic leaves will turn brown and dry out when it is time to harvest. As harvest time approaches, stop watering garlic to prevent bulbs from molding. Gently dig soil around the bulb to check if it is fully formed. Do not rinse harvested garlic. The papery skin must dry out properly to ensure curing for longer storage life.

KALE and COLLARDS

Brassica oleracea, Acephala group

Culture

Kale and closely-related collards are leafy green members of the *Brassica* family. Annual vegetables, they can be grown year-round; sweetest flavor is attained in the cooler months of fall, winter, and spring. Both kale and collards are quite frost-tolerant and are usually harvestable throughout the winter in Portland. Collards can be more heat-tolerant than kale, making them a winner in the summer garden. This hardy leafy green needs a full sun location, with moderately fertile well-drained soil. Varieties of kale are diverse in texture and color.

Jolie's favorite varieties

I enjoy Nero Di Toscana, an 18th century heirloom kale from Italy, also known as Black Palm or Lacinato kale. For curly kales, dark purple Redbor, green Winterbor, and the aptly named Dwarf Blue Curled Scotch are winter-hardy, beautiful, and tasty. I enjoy Red Russian, also known as Ragged Jack, a Siberian heirloom with purple stems and flat-toothed green leaves introduced to Canada in 1885. For collards, I consistently grow Champion.

Planting kale and collards

Kale and collards can be planted from starts or direct-seeded in the garden. I recommend planting in the early spring, March-April, for a spring/summer harvest and again in August for a fall/winter harvest. I have had good success planting kale and collards in a partial sun location receiving about 4 to 6 hours of direct sunlight per day. Plants need to be spaced 2 to 3 feet apart to ensure good ventilation and prevent disease and pest troubles.

Kale and collards care

Kale and collards are moderate feeders and appreciate being planted in soil rich in compost and fertilizer. Continue to apply organic vegetable fertilizer at regular intervals throughout the growing season. Provide consistent average watering and evenly moist soil with good drainage.

Pests and disease

Kale and collards are super delicious and nutritious, are pretty ornamental plants, and do well in the cool Portland weather. Unfortunately, they are plagued by a variety of pests and fungal diseases. Remember, they are members of the large and popular *Brassica* family, and a 4-year rotation is crucial in preventing pests and disease. Common pests are aphids, cabbage moths, and slugs. Apply organic slug bait about every 2 weeks to prevent slugs. Aphids are less active during the cooler temperatures of winter. During the active growing season, attract ladybugs and spray off/squish aphids from undersides of leaves and tender new growth. See Chapter 4 for more troubleshooting tips.

KOHLRABI

Brassica oleracea

Culture

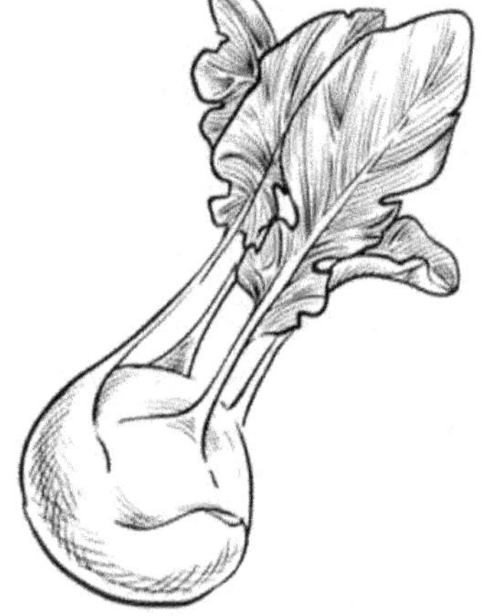

Kohlrabi is a member of the diverse *Brassica oleracea* family. It is a relatively uncommon vegetable in the garden and in the kitchen. Kohlrabi is a descendent of wild cabbage and is sometimes called "German Turnip." The word kohlrabi comes from German, meaning "Turnip Cabbage," but kohlrabi does not taste at all like a spicy turnip, it tastes more like a broccoli stem. I once saw this unusual and delicious vegetable described as a cross between jicama, broccoli, radish, and collards. Kohlrabi is crunchy, sweet, and mild tasting. All parts of the kohlrabi plant are edible—the "bulb," stems, and leaves—and they can all be eaten raw or cooked. Kohlrabi is delicious steamed, baked, roasted, in soups, and raw in salads.

Kohlrabi can be purple or green skinned with white flesh and is an odd looking plant. The part we eat looks like a bulb sitting on the soil surface. It is actually an engorged stem, not a tuber or root. The bulbous part we eat is surrounded by two layers of stiff leaves that are attached in a rosette, like cabbage. Long leafy greens shoot out from the top of the bulb.

Jolie's favorite varieties

Early Purple Vienna, Early White Vienna, Konan, Korist, and Superschmelz.

Planting kohlrabi

Kohlrabi is best planted from direct seeding. Plant seeds 1/4 inch deep and space 1 inch apart. When plants have 2 sets of true leaves, thin the plants to 6 inches apart. Kohlrabi can also be planted from seedlings. Plant kohlrabi during March and April. Avoid planting during May and June because plants maturing during the hot weather of summer produce woody dry bulbs. Kohlrabi can be planted again in late August for a fall and winter harvest.

Kohlrabi care

Kohlrabi is an easy to grow plant, if planted in the correct cool temperatures. It is a light feeder and only requires fertile soil with no supplement fertilization. Mature kohlrabi plants planted in late August for a fall and winter harvest are frost tolerant, and the cool weather brings out sweeter flavor.

Pests and Disease

As a member of the *Brassica* family, aphids, cabbage moths, flea beetles, and slugs can trouble kohlrabi. Practicing a 4-year crop rotation is very important. See Chapter 4 for more information.

Harvesting kohlrabi

Spring-planted kohlrabi should be harvested before the hot temperatures of summer. It is ready to harvest approximately 60 days from planting, when "bulbs" are 2 to 4 inches in diameter. In summer, this golf ball sized "bulb" will be more tender than larger "bulbs." Late summer planted kohlrabi can be harvested throughout the winter with bulbs growing as large as 8 to 10 inches in diameter.

LEEKS

Allium ampeloprasum

Culture

Leeks are tasty members of the allium family with a sweeter, milder flavor than onions. These cool season annual vegetables are frost hardy and require a long growing season. Leeks can be fall or spring planted in a full-sun location with fertile, well-drained soil. Harvest baby leeks or full mature size leeks.

Jolie's favorite varieties

I'm a big fan of two types of leeks: Bandit and Giant Musselburgh, otherwise known as Scotch Flag, an heirloom Scottish variety from the 1880s.

Planting leeks

Plant leeks from starts in the garden March through May. Direct seed leeks in the garden in April and May, when the soil has warmed to at least 50 degrees. In my experience, growing leeks from starts is more successful. Overwintering leek varieties can be planted in August and September to harvest the following spring.

Leek care

Leeks are moderate feeders and like consistent deep watering. Apply an organic vegetable fertilizer at planting time and at regular intervals throughout the growing season. Leeks can be blanched by hilling up soil around the base of the plant.

Pests and disease

In my experience, leeks are mostly pest and disease free.

Harvesting leeks

Depending on the variety and growing season, leeks are generally ready for harvest around 80-100 days from transplant. You can harvest leeks when they are 1/2 inch in diameter. Leeks are cold-hardy plants that can stay in the garden during winter in the Portland climate. If temperatures drop below 20 degrees, all leeks can be harvested or mulched in the garden to extend the harvest season.

LETTUCE

Lactuca sativa

Culture

Lettuce is a cool season annual vegetable that prefers the mild temperatures of spring and fall. Select heat tolerant varieties for a summer harvest. Cold tolerant varieties remain harvestable in mild winters. Countless varieties of lettuce are grouped by type: butterhead, looseleaf, romaine, and crisphead. Lettuce can be grown in a full sun or partial sun (at least 5 hours) location, in well-drained soil. Lettuce is not picky and is an easy vegetable to grow in ground, in raised beds, or in containers. In my opinion, lettuce is a lovely ornamental plant sporting impressive colors and textures.

Jolie's favorite varieties

Some of my favorite colorful lettuce varieties are Continuity, Flashy butter oak, Drunken Woman Frizzy Headed, Red Sails, Merlot, Devil's Tongue, Flashy Trout's Back, and Lolla Rossa.

Planting lettuce

Begin planting lettuce in March after risk of frost, when soil temperatures have warmed to at least 40 degrees. Lettuce can be planted from seeds or starts continually from March through September. Take a break from planting lettuce during the hottest time of summer. Lettuce seeds should be sown very shallow, at about 1/8 inch deep. To ensure a continual harvest of lettuce, succession plant every 2 to 3 weeks.

Lettuce care

Lettuce is a light feeder and does not require supplemental fertilizing after initial planting. Lettuce is made primarily of water and benefits from consistent moderate watering.

Pests and disease

Lettuce is an easy vegetable to grow that is mostly pest- and disease-free. In my experience, slugs enjoy munching lettuce, especially the newest seedlings. Slugs can mow down an entire lettuce patch overnight, so consistent application of slug bait is key. Powdery mildew can sometimes be a problem. See Chapter 4 for troubleshooting tips.

Harvesting lettuce

For best flavor and moist leaves, harvest lettuce during the cool of morning or evening. Harvesting baby lettuce leaves can begin in a few short weeks after planting. Using the cut-and-come-again method, you harvest a handful of leaves about 3/4 of an inch from the soil line. In about another 3 to 4 weeks, the plants will regenerate a new round of leaves. Lettuce can also be harvested by the entire head by cutting off the plant at soil level. Lettuce will bolt with temperature spikes. Once lettuce bolts, the flavor becomes very bitter. Watch the forecast and harvest entire heads of lettuce when temperatures are rising to the upper 80s.

MELONS and WATERMELONS

Cucumis melo
Cucumis lanatus

Culture

Melons and watermelons are heat-loving plants that require hot temperatures and a long summer growing season. Neither factors are characteristic of our summer climate in the Portland metro area. The keys to successfully growing melons in our area are waiting to plant until air and soil temperatures have really warmed up, using season extension techniques, and planting short season varieties.

Many of us are familiar with watermelon, cantaloupe, and honeydew melons. This diverse group of annual fruit we grow in our vegetable gardens is a member of the *Cucurbitaceae* family, along with squash and pumpkins, most closely related to cucumbers. An ancient crop, melons originated in the Middle East and Northeastern Africa. Melons are cultivated and enjoyed all over the world. There are many types of melon, each with a variety of colors, shapes, and sizes.

Melons are large vining plants with tendrils that need space to spread out in the garden. Recently compact "mini melon" varieties have been bred as great solutions for containers and small space gardens. I have grown "Sugar Pot" watermelon and "Tasty Bites" Charentais melon in large containers.

Jolie's favorite varieties

Amy, Minnesota Midget, Mini Love, Snow Leopard, Sugar Pot, Tasty Bites, and Tigger.

Planting melons

Melons thrive in a full sun location with hot temperatures, fertile soil, and a neutral pH. They are heavy feeders, so amend your soil well with compost and lime, and apply an organic granular fertilizer prior to planting. Plant melons from seeds or seedlings in the garden throughout the month of June, when soil temperatures are consistently above 65 degrees and night temperatures are consistently above 55 degrees. Melon plants will not tolerate any cool temperatures. Use black or red plastic mulch to warm the soil and a frost blanket or low tunnel to keep plants warm.

Seeds or seedlings should be planted in hills of soil 4 feet apart from each other. Seeds are planted 1/2 inch deep.

Melon care

Melons are heavy feeders and need monthly application of organic granular fertilizer. Midsummer, when plants are blooming, begin applying a liquid bloom and fruit fertilizer. At midsummer, pinch the growing ends off of all shoots and remove baby melons to encourage the plants to concentrate their energy into ripening the larger melons. Melon plants need consistent moderate watering throughout the growing season.

Melon plants can be grown up a sturdy trellis. I have successfully used an A-frame structure for melons and cucumbers grown in raised beds. This picks the fruits up off the ground to prevent them from rotting while resting on the soil surface.

Pests and disease

A variety of fungal diseases can trouble melon plants, most often powdery mildew. Powdery mildew can be prevented with crop rotation and by avoiding overhead watering. It can be treated with foliar and soil application of compost tea. Please see Chapter 4 for more information.

Harvesting melons

Since melons are such a diverse group, each type of melon will have its own indicators of harvestable maturity. Note the date you planted, and begin checking melon plants at the days to maturity. Melons and watermelons will not mature off the vine, so give them plenty of time on the plant. Melons should be picked during the cool hours of the morning.

Cantaloupes will easily slip from the vine and have a crack around the stem when mature. With other types of melons, check the leaf where the fruit is attached to the vine. This leaf will start to yellow when the melon is ripe. Watermelons are ready to harvest when the tendril closest to the fruit is dry and brown, the stem color becomes dull, the spot resting on the soil turns from white to yellow, and the melon gives a hollow sound when lightly thumped. Honeydew melons indicate they are ripe when their skin color lightens, hairs on the outer skin easily fall off, and the end of the fruit smells sweet. Honeydew and Charentais type melons must be cut from their vine.

ONIONS and SCALLIONS

Allium cepa

Culture

Onions are intertwined indispensably with our cooking. Most onions are a biennial bulb, grown as an annual plant. Onions are grouped into three main types: bulbing, bunching, and multiplier. Most of us are familiar with bulbing and bunching onions. Bulbing onions include storage onions like the common red and yellow onions, cipollini types, and sweet onions like Walla Walla. Bunching onions are the true scallions/green onions. Multiplier onions are an interesting group that forms a cluster of underground bulbs from each single bulb planted.

Jolie's favorite varieties

With the multitude types of onions available, it is hard to pick my favorite. I grow a lot of scallion/bunching type onions and prefer Summer Island, a Japanese bunching variety, and colorful Deep Purple. Evergreen Hardy White is very cold-tolerant, so it is a perfect choice for the winter garden. Walla Wallas are my favorite sweet onion variety that grows fantastically here in the Willamette Valley. Yellow-skinned Ailsa Craig, a Scottish heirloom from 1887, produces large two-pound onions. For Italian cipollini onions, you can't beat white skinned Bianca di Maggio for mild taste. The intriguing Egyptian walking onions are hardy perennial plants that produce bulbs underground and clusters of bulblets at the top of each seed stalk. Walking onions get their name because the onion stalks will bend to the ground and take root themselves, producing more plants from season to season.

Planting onions

Depending on the type, onions can be planted from seeds, bunches, or sets during the spring or fall. Onion plants thrive in a full sun location with well-fertilized, sandy/loamy light soil. To ensure success growing onions in Portland, plant long-day or day-neutral varieties. Bulbing type onions are photoperiodic plants, meaning they regulate their stages of growth by the day length and will only develop bulbs if the length of day is just right. Northern or long-day varieties form bulbs when the days are 14-16 hours long. Day-neutral varieties should develop bulbs when day length is 12-14 hours. To ensure successful gardening in Portland, only plant northern or day neutral varieties.

Select a full sun, well-draining location with light, sandy loam soil rich in organic matter. Plant bulbing onion varieties in fall or spring from "sets." Sets are small dried onion bulbs ready to plant. Bulbing onions can also be planted from soilless "bunches." These are live onion plants fall-planted on a nursery farm and dug in spring then sent to retail nurseries to plant in your garden. I have had really good success in the early spring planting Walla Walla onions from bunches. You can also plant bunching onions from starts sold as tray packs in the spring. However, bulbing type onions take so long to grow—100 to 150 days from transplant—I think it is more successful to plant sets and bunches than tray packs. Scallions/bunching onions can be planted from seeds or starts in both the fall and spring. They are quicker to grow and are harvestable around 60 days. Multiplier and walking onions are best planted in the fall and have a very long growing season of about 250 days.

Onion care

Onions are moderate feeders and appreciate regular applications of organic fertilizer. Onions develop larger bulbs dependent upon the amount of leafy green top growth attained before bulb development begins. Promote lush top growth by ensuring a full sun location, rich soil, regular fertilizing, and consistent moderate watering. Once bulbs begin development, further top growth ends.

Pests and disease

In my experience, onions are mostly pest and disease free. Onion thrips, aphids, and fungal diseases can bother allium family plants. Practice a 4-year crop rotation for all allium family plants.

Harvesting onions

Harvest entire scallions/green onions at about 60 days from seeding or transplanting. Any bulbing variety of onion can also be used as a scallion/green onion by harvesting immature plants. Bulbing onions will signal they are nearing maturity when their tops begin to turn yellow and dry and fall over. When this happens, cease watering onion plants so the bulb's protective paper can form.

When about half the onion tops have fallen over, push over the remainder, and wait about 1 week to harvest all of the bulbs. To ensure longer storage life, cure bulbing onions to toughen up their skins. Cure bulbs by laying them in a warm (75-80 degrees), shaded, dry, well-ventilated location for 1 week.

PARSNIPS

Pastinanca sativa

Culture

Along with celery and fennel, parsnips are members of the carrot family. This annual vegetable is grown for their very long, sweet white root. Parsnips taste sweetest when nipped by a few frosts. With a long growing season of 120 days, parsnips are best planted from seed in the late spring to early summer for a fall and winter harvest. Parsnips are one of my favorite vegetables, and I eat them daily all fall and winter, enjoying them roasted, in chunky stews, and pureed in creamy soup. Parsnips fresh from the garden are sweet and tender, unlike the bland, tough woody roots I sometimes find at the grocery store. It's unfortunate parsnips are not a more popular vegetable!

Jolie's favorite varieties

In my winter garden, you'll find Gladiator or Javelin parsnips.

Planting parsnips

Select a full sun location and prepare the bed by deeply working soil with compost and sand. Only prepare soil when it is dry. Working in wet soil causes compaction that spells death for deeply rooted parsnips, growing 8-12 inches long. Plant parsnips by direct seeding into the garden in June and July, when soil temperature is 55-75 degrees. Seeds are shallowly planted at 1/2 inch deep and are slow to germinate—sometimes taking up to 4 weeks. Cover the seedbed with vermiculite, sand, peat, or well-sifted compost to prevent soil crusting, and keep evenly moist at all times.

Parsnip care

Parsnips are light feeders. High nitrogen found in manure and a lot of fertilizers can cause hairy and misshapen forked roots. Like carrots, parsnips need consistent watering and evenly moist soil throughout the growing season. Overwatering can cause cracked roots.

Pests and disease

Like other members of the carrot family, carrot rust fly maggots and fungal disease can bother parsnips. In my experience, parsnips are mostly pest and disease free.

Harvesting parsnips

These long roots take about 120 days to mature; once mature, they can be dug at any time throughout the winter. Their sweet flavor is enhanced by a couple of frosts. Parsnips can remain in the ground throughout mild winters to be harvested as needed.

PEAS

Pisum sativum

Culture

Peas are members of the diverse and nutritious legume family. A hardy cool season annual vegetable, peas are spring and fall planted. Peas are categorized into three types: snap peas, snow peas, and shelling peas. Several parts of the pea plant can be harvested: entire pods of snow and snap types, the plump seeds of shelling types, delicate new growth tendrils, and even the

pretty edible flowers. **Caution:** Do not confuse edible peas with ornamental flowering sweet peas *Lathyrus odoratus*. All parts of ornamental flowering sweet peas are poisonous.

Like all members of the legume family, peas help fix nitrogen in the garden. The pea plant forms a symbiotic relationship with rhizobial bacteria that remove nitrogen from the air to be accumulated in plant roots. The helpful nitrogen is then converted into a usable form in the garden soil. Peas are mostly disease and pest free, and since they promote nitrogen fixing in the soil, they don't need to be rotated.

Jolie's favorite varieties

My tried and true snow pea is Oregon Sugar Pod II, with good yields and great disease resistance. Golden Sweet from India has flat sunshine yellow pods. Some of my favorite sugar snap type peas are Super Sugar Snap, Sugar Sprint, and Sugar Ann.

Tom Thumb, an English heirloom pea introduced to the United States mid-19th century, is a dwarf variety that grows fantastically in containers. For shelling peas, I like Alderman and Green Arrow. Blue-Podded Shelling Pea is a Dutch heirloom that sports exquisite purple pods.

Planting peas

Peas thrive in a full sun location. In my experience, they can grow successfully in a slightly less sunny location of my garden, receiving around 6 hours of direct sunlight and bright indirect light the remainder of the day. I have seen several sources recommend planting peas from seed in February in the Portland area, supporting the old saying "Plant peas by President's Day." I do agree that peas are one of the very first vegetables to go in the cool-season garden, however, in my experience, in February the Portland area garden soil is still way too cold and too wet to promote good germination of pea seeds. I prefer the suggestion of "Plant peas around St. Patrick's Day," and I annually plant peas in March.

Plant peas February through May for an early summer harvest. Peas may be planted from seed or starts. Seeds are quick to germinate, in two to three weeks, when planted 1-inch deep in soil warmed to at least 45 degrees. To ensure adequate populations of rhizobial bacteria, purchase a bag of inoculant from your local nursery, and coat pea seeds immediately prior to planting. Once you've used inoculant you won't need to repeat in the same garden soil area. Peas grow in both vine and bush varieties. Be sure to plant vining varieties with a trellis, tripod, or stakes.

Pea care

Peas are light feeders and do not require supplemental fertilizing while growing.

When planting peas by seed, keep the seed bed evenly moist until germination. Pea plants then need less watering until they develop flowers. Once flowering, resume consistent watering.

Pests and disease

In my experience, peas are an easy vegetable to grow that is mostly pest and disease free.

Harvesting peas

Most peas are ready to harvest around 60-70 days from transplant or seed germination. Harvest peas frequently to ensure plants keep producing. Sugar and shelling peas can be harvested when peas begin to swell. If pea pods are left on the plant too long, they become tough and starchy. Pea shoots/tendrils can be harvested once the plants have reached 3 feet tall by pinching off the top 6 inches. Pea shoots with flowers are tender and delicious in salads and stir fries; however, remember that when you harvest the tendrils, you do so at the expense of growing mature peas. Peas do not like hot weather, and in my experience, they are done producing by July. To ensure another harvest in fall, pull up spring-planted plants, compost, and plant new seeds again in August.

PEPPERS

Capsicum annum

Culture

Peppers are an ancient plant originating in Mexico and Central and South America. Peppers are classified as sweet or hot and come in a colorful array of shapes, sizes, and flavors. A member of the *Solanaceae* or "nightshade" family, peppers are the fruiting part of the plant—all other parts are toxic.

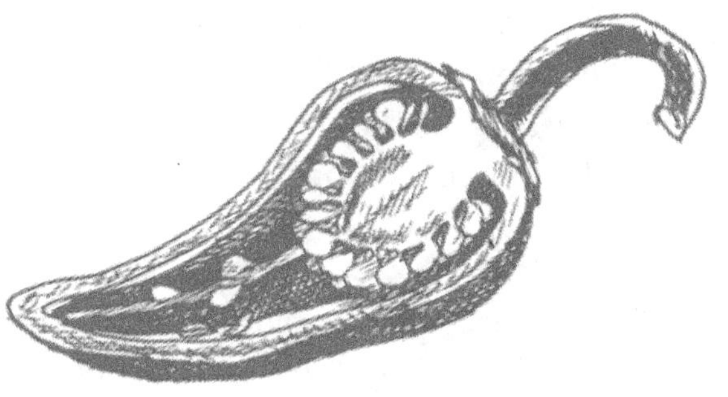

Peppers require at least 7 hours of direct sun and thrive in hot temperatures with dry, long growing seasons. Without this heat, the fruit will not develop and ripen. The key to a successful harvest in our cooler climate and shorter summer growing season is to choose short season varieties and wait to plant until the temperatures have warmed. Peppers grow slowly in cool soil and air temperatures, so do not jump the gun on planting. The plants will set fruit best between 65-85 degrees F. Peppers can be successfully grown in ground, raised beds, or in containers in our climate. Typically, the fruit will not have the searing hot flavor of peppers grown in hotter regions.

Jolie's favorite varieties

Alma Paprika, Golden Star, Gourmet, Gypsy, Healthy, Italian Pepperoncini, Italian Sweet, and Jimmy Nardello.

Planting peppers

Peppers like slightly acidic soil, so amending our native ground soil with compost works great. Well-draining soil is optimal so plants do not dampen off in waterlogged cool soil.

Wait to plant peppers until night temperatures are consistently above 55 degrees, typically after May 15. Pepper growth is stunted when temperatures fall below 55 degrees, so keep plants protected with a water-filled cloche, a frost blanket, or a cold frame. Due to the short growing season, peppers must be planted in the garden by seedlings, not seeds. Space plants 18 inches apart.

Pepper care

Peppers are heavy feeders and require monthly applications of organic granular fertilizer throughout the growing season. During mid-summer, begin adding a liquid bloom and fruit fertilizer. Peppers require extra calcium and phosphorus for highest yields. This can be found in garden lime, bone meal, fish bone meal, and rock phosphate.

When pepper plants are young, keep them consistently moderately watered. Consistent watering assists in preventing blossom end rot. Mature pepper plants are drought tolerant and prefer drier conditions.

Pests and disease

Flea beetles, aphids, spider mites, and slugs can prey on pepper plants. Like other members of the *Solanaceae* family, peppers can be prone to blossom end rot and fungal diseases like blight, tobacco mosaic virus, and verticillium wilt. Crop rotation of this entire plant family is important in preventing fungal disease. For more information, see Chapter 4. In my experience, pepper plants aren't troubled by fungal disease or pests. Instead, they struggle to develop and ripen fruit in our cooler climate.

Harvesting peppers

Note the date you planted, and watch for days to maturity. In general, peppers are fully ripe and have the best flavor when they reach their mature size and have turned their mature color: yellow, orange, red, or purple. Any type of sweet pepper can be harvested at full size, while still green, to use as green peppers. Cut each fruit from the plant with 1 inch of stem.

POTATOES

Solanum tuberosum

Culture

Potatoes are a member of the large *Solanum/* nightshade family. This tuberous rooted vegetable is grown as an annual and harvested for its tasty, starchy underground tubers. All other parts of the potato plant, leaves, and flowers are poisonous.

Potatoes come in a wealth of beautiful skin and flesh colors. White, yellow, pink, red, purple, and brown potatoes are all fun and relatively easy to grow with huge yields. Spring planted, potato varieties are harvestable early, mid, and late season. Planting several varieties ensures a continual harvest of potatoes.

If you have ever taken one of my gardening classes, you will know that growing potatoes is a favorite in my family. When I met my husband, he was enthusiastic about growing two things: potatoes and strawberries. Since his birthday and St. Patrick's day are both in March, it has become an annual tradition for my Irishman to plant potatoes on his birthday.

Jolie's favorite varieties

Every year, I like to grow a few favorite varieties and trial at least one variety that is new to my garden.

My favorite yellow skin/flesh varieties are German Butterball, Yukon Gold, and Yukon Gem. For red skin/white flesh, I like Dark Red Norland. In the blue skin/flesh category, Purple Majesty is stunning and tasty. I've grown several varieties of fingerling, and hands down my favorite is Russian Banana for superior yields and excellent flavor.

Planting potatoes

Potatoes require a full sun location with fertile, loose, well-drained, slightly acidic soil high in phosphorus and low in nitrogen. Begin planting potatoes in March, around 3 weeks before the average last frost date, when soil temperatures are between 55 to 70 degrees. Always plant potatoes from certified seed potatoes available from a local or mail order nursery. Never plant potatoes from grocery store potatoes, as they are almost always treated with a sprouting inhibitor to retard shoot growth for longer shelf life. This is no good for the home gardener and will result in low yields. Organic potatoes from the grocery store may not be treated, but they may carry diseases that you do not want to risk contaminating your garden soil. Certified seed potatoes are meticulously monitored to be disease free.

Small seed potatoes can be planted whole. Larger tubers should be cut with a clean knife into several smaller pieces, each with 1 to 2 strong sprouts called "eyes." Once cut, let seed potato pieces heal over to prevent rot: dust them in garden sulphur and place in a paper bag in a dark, dry, cool place for 24 hours.

Plant seed potatoes 4 to 6 inches deep. For best yield, I highly recommend the hilling method. This is easiest to do in a raised bed dedicated for potatoes, or in a container. We grow potatoes in several large food-grade plastic storage bins. You can also use commercially made potato grow bags. In about 2 to 3 weeks, sprouts will emerge from the soil. When the green leafy stems are about 8-12 inches high, cover them halfway up with fresh soil. You can "hill" soil around the stems, or, in a container or dedicated raised bed, it is easy to cover the stems evenly with fresh soil. Continue this hilling process 3 to 4 times during the growing season. Hilling/mounding soil at intervals will ensure potato plants grow multiple levels of potatoes from their covered stems.

In my experience, 1 to 2 seed potatoes can yield about 50 potatoes!

Potato care

Potatoes can be fertilized at regular intervals until blooming begins, and then stop fertilizing. Be sure to use a fertilizer high in phosphorus and low in nitrogen, like bone meal and rock phosphate. Water regularly when the soil dries out.

Pests and disease

Remember studying the Irish Potato Famine in school? A fungal disease called blight wiped out an entire nation's primary food crop. Fungal diseases and potatoes are no joke, even for the small urban gardener. Potatoes, along with all other members of the *Solanum*/nightshade family, require a 4-year crop rotation for best prevention of disease and pests. Because potatoes are susceptible to blight, wilt, scab, potato beetle, potato worms, and a host of other problems, crop rotation and organic gardening methods for soil health are your best allies. In my garden, I exclusively grow potatoes in containers so I can conserve limited raised bed space and annually dispose of soil when harvesting. I spread used soil around ornamental gardens or use it in containers growing flowers, plants not susceptible to blight. Containers are cleaned with a mild vinegar solution and refilled with fresh soil and compost for the new growing season.

Harvesting potatoes

At planting time, take note of days to maturity for your potato varieties. The days to maturity varies between potato varieties and will assist you in preparing for an approximate harvest date. For example, Yukon Gold potatoes have 65 days to maturity, Dark Red Norland have 80 days to maturity, and Russian Banana fingerling potatoes have 90-100 days to maturity.

You will know when your potato plants are nearing harvest when their green stalks and leaves begin to turn yellow and fall over. You can break off the stalks at soil level, but leave potato tubers in place. At this time, stop watering your potato plants and let the tubers rest in the soil undisturbed for 2 weeks. This will help the potato skin to "set" and will increase their storage life.

To harvest your potatoes, carefully dig in soil, being careful not pierce any tubers with your shovel. Thoroughly remove all tubers from garden soil, as any potatoes left behind will sprout new plants in subsequent years. Store your potato tubers in a cool, dry, dark place out of sunlight.

RADISHES

Raphanus sativus

Culture

Diminutive, crunchy radishes are members of the *Brassica/*
crucifer family and are one of the easiest and quickest annual
vegetables to grow. In early spring, their peppery taste and bright
color is a welcome addition to salads. Radishes are round or
cylindrical and come in shades of white, pink, red, purple, and
green. Preferring cool weather, they can be planted in spring
and fall.

Jolie's favorite varieties

Round Cherry Belle and elongated French Breakfast are my favorite standard red salad radish varieties. Easter Egg is a bright blend of red, pink, purple, and white radishes. Watermelon is a variety with white skin and a surprising pink-purple center. Tapered and slim White Icicle has solid white skin and flesh. The unique and uncommon Rat-Tailed

Radish is an heirloom native to South Asia that is grown for its spicy and crispy edible seedpods instead of the roots.

Planting radishes

Select a full to partial sun location with loose well-draining soil. Plant radishes from seed 1/2 inch deep directly into the garden during March through June, when soil temperature warms up to 45 degrees. Take a break from planting radishes during the hottest months of summer. Begin planting again in late August through September for a fall harvest.

Radish care

Radishes are light feeders and do not need any supplemental fertilizing. Plants have small short roots with shallow root systems that require regular consistent watering. Radishes are stressed by dry soil and will grow slowly, developing a pithy texture. Radishes will bolt in high temperatures, turning their roots long and woody rather than round and juicy.

Pests and disease

Radishes are so quick growing that they are rarely bothered by pests and disease. Occasionally, flea beetles and aphids are troublesome on greens. Remember that radishes are members of the *Brassica*/crucifer family and should be included in a 4-year rotation. See Chapter 4 for more details on rotation methodology.

Harvesting radishes

Radishes are one of the quickest vegetable crops to harvest. They are mature and ready to harvest in as little as 3 weeks from planting date. When radishes are 1 inch across or have reached their specified days to maturity, begin harvesting and store in the refrigerator. Radishes do not benefit from being left in the ground. They do not improve with age, and instead turn woody and unpalatable.

RUTABAGA and TURNIP

Brassica napus
B. rapa

Culture

Rutabaga and turnips are members of the large *Brassica* family and are eaten primarily for their roots. Their greens are also edible. They are cool season crops. Turnips are grown in both spring and fall. Rutabagas are a staple of the winter vegetable garden, planted in mid-summer for a fall and winter harvest.

Rutabagas—also referred to as "Swedes"—are a cross between cabbage and turnip. Their purple skin covers a creamy yellow flesh that is wonderful roasted, baked, mashed, pureed, and used in soups and stews. Rutabagas are larger, sweeter, and milder than turnips. Turnips have a distinct spicy taste, particularly the older, larger roots.

Jolie's favorite varieties

Rutabaga: American Purple Top and Joan.
Turnip: Golden Ball, Hakurel, and Purple Top White Globe.

Planting rutabaga and turnip

Both vegetables are direct-seeded in the garden. They can tolerate a wide variety of soil types, though they will produce the best roots in loose soil amended with organic matter.

Plant turnip seeds in April and May for a late spring to early summer harvest. Plant turnip seeds again in late August for a fall and winter harvest. Plant rutabaga seeds in July for a fall and winter harvest. Ideal soil temperature for germination is 55 to 75 degrees F. Plant seeds 1/4 to one 1/2 deep and space 1 to 2 inches apart. Thin seedlings to 6 inches apart.

Rutabaga and turnip care

Keep the seedbed evenly moist to ensure maximum germination. Plants need consistent moderate watering throughout their growth. Both crops are light feeders and only require an application of organic granular fertilizer at planting time.

Pests and disease

Like other members of the *Brassica* family, aphids, cabbage moths, flea beetles, and slugs can bother rutabagas and turnips. Rotation of this entire family is very important. See Chapter 4 for more information.

Harvesting rutabaga and turnip

Turnips can be harvested at about 50 days from germination, when at a small golf ball size—for sweeter flavor—or at mature tennis ball size. Rutabagas have a sweeter flavor when touched with a frost. They can be harvested starting around 90-100 days from germination. Both crops are hardy down to 20 degrees and can be left in the ground most of winter for harvesting as needed.

SALAD GREENS

Culture

Salad greens are a large group of different plants harvested for their greens, typically used raw in salads. Most salad greens prefer cooler weather and grow stupendously during the spring and fall here in Portland. I could write an entire book about salad greens. Salad greens go above and beyond the usual suspects of lettuce, mesclun mix, and spinach. Some of my favorite salad greens are arugula, cress, dandelion, escarole, endive, mache, purslane, orach, and radicchio. When creating a beautiful spring salad, I add handfuls of freshly harvested baby lettuce, beet greens, chard, herb foliage, and edible flowers. Some bitter, some peppery, some mild—all of these salad greens provide different color, texture, and taste to the salad. Overall, they are also really easy to grow.

Jolie's favorite varieties

There are two main types of annual arugula grown as salad greens: wild arugula (*Eruca vesicaria*) and salad arugula/rocket (*Rucola selvatica*). For salad arugula, I like Roquette and Apollo. For summer growing, I like heat-tolerant Astro. For wild arugula, I like the very winter-hardy Sylvetta.

Other favorite greens include Palla Rossa radicchio, Golden purslane, Double Purple orach, Vit mache, Early Wonder beets for baby greens, Broadleaf Batavian escarole, and Rhodos and Benefine endives.

Planting salad greens

Select a full to partial sun location with well-draining average soil. Plant salad greens from seed directly into the garden during March through May, when soil temperatures have warmed to 50 degrees. Follow seed packet instructions for planting depth, days to germination, and days to maturity. Successively plant salad green seeds every 2 weeks during spring for a continual harvest. Most salad greens will tolerate a light frost but will bolt and develop bitter flavor when temperatures become warm. Ideal air temperature for salad greens flavor and growth is 60-70 degrees. Start planting salad greens again in August and September for a fall harvest. Most salad greens are compact and do well grown in containers.

Salad green care

Salad greens are light feeders and do not need supplemental fertilization. For most salad greens beds, I use only liquid seaweed as a fertilizer at planting time. Frequent watering to keep the seed bed evenly moist is required for good germination. Salad greens require consistent moderate watering throughout their growing season.

Pests and disease

In my experience, most salad greens are relatively disease and pest free plants that are easy to grow in containers, raised beds, or in-ground gardens. Be watchful for slugs as they love the tender new growth of all salad greens and can mow down a bed of seedlings overnight.

Harvesting salad greens

Read seed packets for dates to maturity for each variety of salad green planted. Remember, flavors are best during the cooler temperatures. If temperatures above 70 degrees are predicted, harvest salad greens to prevent bolting. Harvest salad greens in the cooler temperatures of morning and evening. Rinsing in cold water can refresh harvested salad greens. To really enjoy the flavor and texture of fresh spring salad greens, I only lightly dress with homemade herbal vinaigrette.

SHALLOTS

Allium cepa **var.** *ascalonicum*

Culture

Shallots are another tasty member of the allium family, with a richer, milder flavor than onions and garlic. These tiny gourmet treasures are expensive to buy at the supermarket and easy for the home gardener to grow. While bulbing type onions and shallots are closely related cousins, shallots form a cluster of small cloves instead of one large bulb. This makes shallots easier to grow than bulbing type onions, and they have a higher yield of tasty tapered cloves. Shallots have a long season to maturity and will yield best when fall planted.

Jolie's favorite varieties

I prefer Dutch Yellow and Holland Red varieties.

Planting shallots

Choose a full sun site with light, loamy, well-drained, rich soil. Amend soil with compost and organic vegetable fertilizer. Plant shallots from bulbs obtained at a local or mail order nursery. Ideal planting time is the same as garlic, in the fall between September and October. Plant bulbs root end down, tapered tip pointing up, only 1 inch deep in prepared soil. Fall planting ensures bulbs develop roots and some leafy green growth before winter sets in. Ensure plenty of leafy green growth by providing a full sun location, adequate spacing, regular watering, and fertilizer.

Shallot care

Shallots have shallow root systems and need consistent watering throughout their growing seasons, but be sure to let soil dry out between watering. Continue to provide fertilizing at regular intervals throughout the spring and summer growing seasons. Like other allium family members, shallots will stop leafy green growth when they are developing underground bulbs. At this time, stop watering shallot plants. This will assist in the bulbs in developing their papery skin, which promotes longer storage life.

Pests and disease

Shallots are mostly disease and pest free, although the same pests and diseases that affect garlic and onions may trouble your shallots. You'll find more information about pests and diseases in Chapter 4.

Harvesting shallots

Like onions and garlic, shallots signal their bulbs are maturing when their leaves turn yellow and begin to fall over. Make sure watering has stopped by this time. Harvest bulbs when all foliage has turned yellow and fallen over. In general, shallots yield 4 to 5 times what was planted. Cure shallots in the same way as onions.

SPINACH

Spinacia oleracea

Culture

Spinach is a member of the same plant family as beets and chard. This annual vegetable, grown for its nutritious leafy greens, favors cool weather and is best grown in the spring or fall. Leaves can be harvested as baby or full size. They are are delicious eaten raw or cooked. Thick succulent leaves hold up better with richer dressing than do more delicate salad greens.

Jolie's favorite varieties

Spinach varieties I prefer include Bloomsdale Savoy, Olympia, and Tyee.

Planting spinach

Select a full or partial sun site with fertile soil. Spinach can be planted from seed or starts during March through May, when soil temperature is between 50-70 degrees. Soil temperature above 80 degrees makes for poor germination. Seeds planted 1/2 inch deep germinate in 1 to 3 weeks, depending on conditions. Successively plant spinach every 2 to 3 weeks through the end of June to ensure a continual harvest. Start planting spinach again in August for a fall harvest.

Spinach care

Spinach is a light feeder and does not need supplemental fertilizing. Often the only fertilizer I provide spinach with is liquid seaweed. Spinach requires consistent watering throughout its growing season. This cool-season plant is stressed by water and temperature fluctuations that cause premature bolting.

Pests and disease

Like beets and chard, leaf miners constantly prey on spinach. Practice 4-year crop rotation and consider organic pest strategies. Be on the watch for slugs, as they favor tender spinach leaves to devour. See Chapter 4 for more info.

Harvesting spinach

Spinach is ready to be harvested in about 50 days from transplanting or germination. Baby spinach greens are ready to be harvested when they are only 3-4 inches. Harvest individual leaves as needed in the cooler times of morning and evening.

SWISS CHARD

Beta vulgaris, Cicica group

Culture

Swiss chard shares the same plant family as spinach and beets, and sometimes goes by the names "leaf beet" or "perpetual spinach." This quick growing cool season biennial vegetable is grown as an annual crop. The colorful, large, leafy greens of chard are more heat tolerant for dependable summer growing than spinach or kale. In mild temperatures, it will overwinter, making chard a great option for year-round harvest. Most folks eat the rumpled leaves of chard that can grow almost two feet long, but they are missing out on the brightly colored 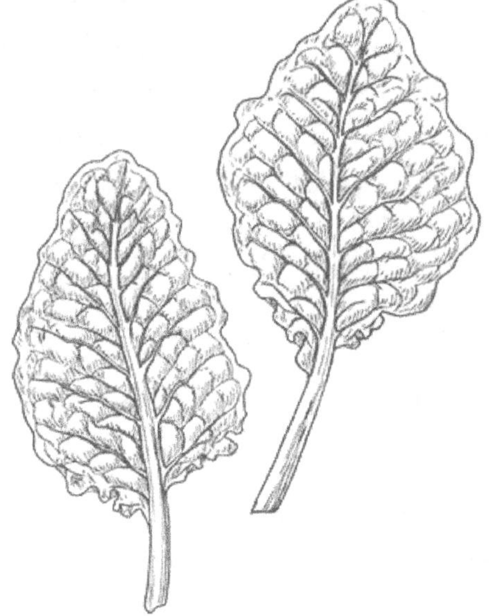 succulent crunchy stems that can be eaten raw or cooked like celery stalks. Swiss chard is an easy-to-grow vegetable and is so colorful and pretty it makes a delightful addition to the ornamental garden.

Jolie's favorite varieties

I love all the bright colors of heirloom Five Color Silverbeet, also called Rainbow Chard. Stems and veins are a brilliant mix of white, yellow, orange, red, and pink.

Planting Swiss chard

Swiss chard prefers a full sun location, though it can grow in partial sun of about 6 hours per day. Plant chard from seed or starts in the spring after risk of last frost, when the soil temperatures have warmed to at least 50 degrees. If conditions are optimal, seeds are usually quick to germinate in less than 2 weeks. Chard planted March through June will yield a harvest by summer. Plant Swiss chard again in July through September for a fall and winter harvest.

Swiss chard care

Swiss chard is a moderate feeder and appreciates regular applications of organic vegetable fertilizer, higher in nitrogen, throughout the growing season. Keep the seed bed consistently moist until germination and provide plants with regular watering throughout their growing season.

Pests and disease

Swiss chard, like its family members spinach and beets, is frequently bothered by leafminers. Aphids, flea beetles, and fungal disease can sometimes bother chard. Be sure to include chard in a 4-year crop rotation. See Chapter 4 for more information on combatting leafminers.

Harvesting Swiss chard

Swiss chard can be harvested as baby greens when the leaves are only a few inches tall. In general, chard is at harvestable maturity around 60 days from transplanting or germination, when leaves are between 12-24 inches long. Individual leaves or entire bunches may be harvested. Harvesting individual leaves will ensure the plant keeps producing. Harvest outer leaves first and leave the center of plant to grow more leaves. Regularly harvesting chard will ensure tender leaves at the peak of flavor. More mature, larger leaves can become leathery, brittle, and tough with stringy stems.

SUMMER SQUASH and ZUCCHINI

Cucurbita spp.

Culture

Summer squash are heat-loving summer grown as annual vegetables that include zucchini, patty pan, and crookneck varieties. Unlike their family members, winter squash and pumpkins, summer squash has tender thin skin and a much shorter shelf life. Summer squash are bountiful producers that require a full sun location, richly amended fertile soil, and lots of space to spread out. Most summer squash are bush varieties and need at least 3 to 4 square feet of growing space per each plant. For small space gardens and even containers, look for new compact varieties like Patio Star zucchini. These plants are so prolific, I usually only grow one variety each summer. Due to their high water content, summer squash and zucchini do not freeze well and need to be eaten fresh.

Jolie's favorite varieties

If I had to choose only one squash variety to grow every year for the rest of my life, there is no doubt it would be the prolific buttery-tasting Sunburst patty pan. Benning's Green Tint is a very pale green patty pan type summer squash. Yellow crookneck is a warty-skinned tasty summer squash. Last year we grew Dixie, a newer variety of summer crookneck squash with smooth skin and sweet tasty flesh, and we had an abundant harvest.

Dark green Black Beauty and ribbed Costata Romanesco are my favorite zucchini varieties. If you have room for an exceptionally large squash vine, consider the intriguing and uncommon Tromboncino. It is an Italian-heirloom summer squash that uniquely rambles on six foot vines, with light green fruits up to 3 feet long. It can be eaten fresh like zucchini, or skin can be cured to preserve like winter squash. Give it room! One year we grew it in our community garden and it took over our entire 4-foot by 10-foot plot!

Planting summer squash and zucchini

Summer squash are heat-loving plants, so please resist temptation to plant them too early in the garden. Wait until soil temperature has risen to at least 65 degrees and night air temperatures are consistently above 55 degrees. In the Portland area, this is typically mid-May through June. Summer squash can be planted from either seeds or starts. If conditions are ideal, seeds will germinate in about 1 week.

Squash and zucchini care

Both vegetables are moderate feeders. They appreciate a good organic fertilizer and well-amended soil at planting time. In the first month of growth, supplemental fertilizing with an all-purpose or higher nitrogen fertilizer will encourage strong leafy green plant growth. Once the plant begins blooming and producing fruit, switch to applications of a "bloom/fruit" type fertilizer higher in phosphorus, like rock phosphate. Squash need moderate watering, and the soil must be kept evenly moist. Be sure to water the soil, not the foliage, as squash is prone to powdery mildew.

Pests and disease

In my experience, summer squash is mostly pest free. The two biggest problems I see are lack of pollination and powdery mildew. Summer squash plants are monoecious, meaning they bear separate female and male flowers on the same plant. For the female flowers to produce fruit, pollen must arrive from the male flowers by an insect pollinator, like bees. You can assist pollination by not using sprays and by planting companion flowers in your garden. If squash family plants are not receiving pollination, the small fruit, sometimes with flower still attached, will fall off the vine. You can hand pollinate your squash family plants by first identifying the male flowers and female flowers. Inside the male flowers is a small cone shape covered in pollen. Inside the female flowers is a flat disc shape covered in pollen. Take a small, clean paint brush or cotton swab, dip into the male flower and coat with pollen, and then apply the pollen inside the female flower. Repeat daily to pollinate every female flower.

Powdery mildew is so common in Portland area gardens. Usually by late summer, most squash family plants will start showing small white spots on their leaves before becoming coated in white, crumbling on the edges, and drying out. See Chapter 4 for excellent strategies to prevent and treat powdery mildew.

Harvesting squash and zucchini

Depending on the variety, summer squash is usually ready to be harvested about 50-60 days from transplant or germination. To encourage plants to continue producing, fruits should be harvested regularly when they are small in size. Large fruits contain larger seeds, have poor flavor, and signal the plants to decrease production. Summer squash plants will not tolerate frost, so all fruits should be harvested by the end of September.

TOMATOES

Lycopersicon lycopersicum

Culture

I once read that tomatoes are the number one garden plant grown in the United States. I have also heard the funny expression "tomatoes are a gateway drug to all kinds of gardening." Indeed, I get more questions from gardeners about growing tomatoes than about growing other plants, and I could easily compose an entire book on it.

Why such obsession with tomatoes? Certainly, there is a seemingly endless quantity of varieties in colors of white, yellow, orange, pink, red, blue/purple, brown, black, and variegated combinations. Tomatoes are a heat-loving annual crop that thrives in long, hot summers. Portland hardly has long hot summers, so to ensure growing success, select a northern variety that reaches harvestable maturity in less than 85 days. Despite our non-optimal growing season, I find tomatoes mostly an easy-to-grow garden favorite.

Tomato plants grow two ways, determinate and indeterminate, and it is important to know which type you are growing. Determinate tomatoes grow compactly and to a certain height, flowering and setting fruit all at the same time. Many determinate tomatoes are 'Roma,' sauce, or paste varieties good for preservation. Indeterminate tomatoes grow on long stems, ripen at variable times throughout the season, and continue to grow and produce until a frost kills the plant. Many indeterminate tomatoes are cherry and slicing types.

Planting tomatoes

Large tomato plants need 2 to 3 square feet between each plant. They require a full sun location with rich, well-amended fertilized soil. Due to the length of time it takes them to reach maturity, tomatoes must be planted from seedlings. If you are wishing to plant tomatoes by seed, start them indoors during January and February. Tomatoes are heat-loving summer plants that will not tolerate cool temperatures or frost. Plant tomato seedlings when night temperatures have warmed to consistently above 55 degrees and soil is warmed to at least 70 degrees. In the Portland area, this is typically between mid-May through mid-June.

Resist the temptation to plant tomatoes too early. If temperatures are too cold, you will not get any jump-start on the growing season by stressing and stunting your plants.

Tomato seedlings can be planted with protection, such as a "wall-of-water" or "kozy-coat" product or cloches. When planting tomatoes, add a calcium source such as a handful each of rock phosphate or bone meal and lime to help prevent blossom end rot. Tomato plants have fuzzy stems that will root and can be planted up to the top 2 sets of leaves. Watering new seedlings with liquid seaweed will encourage root development. All tomato seedlings should have a sturdy large cage installed at planting time. Purchase the largest tomato cage you can find; those wimpy 3-foot tall galvanized cages are not going to cut it. Giving your tomato plants proper support will result in healthier plants and higher yields.

Jolie's favorite varieties

There are thousands of tomato varieties, and through the years I have grown close to fifty different varieties. Heirloom tomato varieties have superior fresh-from-the-garden taste and a diverse palette of colors, shapes, and sizes. Have fun and explore!

Here are some of my favorite dependable and flavorful varieties grouped by type:
Cherry tomatoes: Matt's Wild Cherry, Sungold, Sweet Million, and Yellow Pear.
Slicing tomatoes: Ananas Noire, Lemon Boy, Costoluto Genovese, and Momotaro.
Early tomatoes: Glacier, Oregon Spring, and Siletz.
Paste/sauce tomatoes: Amish Paste and San Marzano.

Tomato care

Tomatoes are heavy feeders and require regular applications of organic fertilizer throughout the growing season. Once tomato plants are flowering and setting fruit, switch from a higher nitrogen fertilizer to a higher phosphorus fertilizer.

During the first month the tomato plants are growing, they should be encouraged to develop lots of lush green growth and a strong healthy plant. Pinch off any flowers at this stage of development. Indeterminate varieties become huge plants with way too many stems. It is important to pinch out suckers in between main branches where they connect with the main stems. This will promote a healthy plant with good air circulation and enough leaves to support photosynthesis, while encouraging development and ripening of fruit in our shorter summer growing season.

Newly planted tomato seedlings need consistent watering until established. Always water deeply and less frequently to develop deeper roots and a plant that is more drought tolerant. In general, established tomato plants are quite drought tolerant and need less water than other garden crops. Overwatering and inconsistent watering leads to cracked fruit and blossom end rot. Around the beginning of September, I completely stop watering my tomato plants and prune off any stems with smaller green fruit to encourage the plant to ripen all its fruit before the colder weather sets in.

Pests and disease

In my experience, tomatoes are generally pest free, though flea beetles and tomato hornworms could be a problem. Tomatoes can be prone to a variety of fungal diseases like blight and blossom end rot, and they can have cracked fruit. Be sure to practice a 4-year crop rotation.

Harvesting tomatoes

Harvest tomatoes when they are fully ripe, and eat them fresh. Cherry tomatoes will be the first to ripen and can be harvested continually throughout the growing season. In my experience, cherry tomatoes are ready by mid-summer, around July. Early varieties of slicers are the next to mature, followed by determinate varieties of sauce tomatoes, and finally, larger slicing varieties. Determinate varieties should be harvested all at once for preservation by freezing, canning, or drying. The bulk of the tomato harvest in Portland is late summer, around August into September. All unripe green fruit can be harvested in September and laid out in a cool dark area to ripen indoors. Never store tomatoes in the refrigerator, as this ruins their flavor and texture.

WINTER SQUASH

Cucurbita spp.

Culture

Winter squash share many of the same characteristics as summer squash, including being heat-loving annual vegetables grown during the summer. Some differences: winter squash require a long growing season, averaging around 100+ days, and they have a hard outer skin that gives them a long shelf life for winter storage of about 3 to 4 months. Their long vining habit, about 4 to 5 square feet, requires even more growing space, which can be a challenge in raised beds or smaller gardens.

Jolie's favorite varieties

My two favorite winter squash that are uncommon in the grocery store are Red Kuri—an orange type of miniature hubbard—and Shokichi Green, which is a miniature kabocha. The most fantastic tasting winter squash soup I've ever made was using a Blue

Hubbard.

Some other beautiful heirloom winter squash varieties that have piqued my interest are Banana Pink Jumbo (sometimes called Candy Roaster), Thelma Sanders Sweet Potato (a cream-color acorn squash), Long Island Cheese, and an Italian heirloom called Marina di Chioggia that is a large, grey-green, bumpy-skinned, turban-shaped squash. Standards in my winter cooking are Waltham Butternut, Bush Delicata, Small Wonder Spaghetti, and Sweet Dumpling.

Planting winter squash

See Summer Squash

Winter squash care

See Summer Squash

Pests and disease

See Summer Squash

Harvesting winter squash

Winter squash should be left on the vine until fully mature, when skins are firm. Cut stem 1 to 2 inches from fruit. For maximum storage time, winter squash should be cured properly. Curing will depend on the variety. General guidelines are to let cut winter squash cure in the garden for about 15 days. If weather is wet, cure winter squash in a warm indoor space for 15 days.

Notes

Notes

11 / A–Z Guide to the Best Herbs for Portland

CULINARY HERBS WERE SOME OF THE first plants I grew in containers when I began gardening in 1995. Adding fresh herbs to cooking and tea elevates their flavor and complexity.

Wandering through the summer garden, I pick the tiny pale pink blossoms of the lemon thyme plant and pop them right into my mouth for a burst of citrus and floral flavors. Gathering a handful of fresh fragrant lemon verbena and apple mint leaves to put in my teapot, pouring over with boiling water for a warming cup of tea, is a simple pleasure I do not take for granted. With delight, I look forward to the seasonal treats of my herb garden. This chapter features a selection of my favorite herbs for growing in Portland area gardens, with specific varieties where applicable.

BASIL

Ocimum basilicum

Culture

Basil is a summer-grown, heat-loving, annual herb. Often associated with Italian and Thai cooking, basil can be successfully grown in the wet cool Portland climate if it is planted at the correct time. That means being patient during our unpredictable late spring and early summer weather.

Jolie's favorite varieties

My favorites include Cinnamon, Genovese, lemon, licorice, Mrs. Burns, purple ruffles, red rubin, Siam Queen Thai, and sweet basil.

Planting basil

Basil detests cold temperatures and soggy soil. This heat-loving plant will perish if night temperatures are below 55 degrees. Typically, I am planting basil plants around the first of June, sometimes later, depending on the weather that year. Due to our short summer growing season, I always plant basil from starts, not seeds.

Basil likes to be planted in well-draining soil with mild fertilizer in a full sun location.

Basil care

For the most abundant harvest of leaves, pinch off the flowers down to the next set of leaves. Weekly tip-pruning throughout the growing season will keep plants bushy rather than leggy and tall. To store fresh basil in the house, I place harvested stems in a glass of water and leave it on the counter to cook with throughout the week. You will notice basil stems will begin to root into water. These can be used to plant new plants in the garden or in a pot for a winter kitchen windowsill garden.

Harvesting basil

The cool and rainy weather of fall will kill summer basil plants. In August and September, I harvest big bunches of basil to freeze for winter use. You can also harvest basil by individual leaves or by pinching off select stems.

CHAMOMILE

German chamomile *Matricaria recutita*
Roman chamomile *Chamaemelum nobile*

Culture

There are two plants called chamomile. Roman chamomile is an upright annual plant with the preferred flavor for chamomile tea. German chamomile is a low growing perennial ground cover that is preferred for medicinal preparations. The second type of chamomile makes a lovely fragrant ground cover and sod alternative. Both types of chamomile grow well in Portland.

Planting chamomile

Chamomile can be grown from seed or starts in a full sun location during the spring. German chamomile will readily self-seed itself and return to the garden each spring. The miniature daisy-like flowers are very attractive to bees and beneficial bugs, and they can be a nice addition to natural-looking bouquets. A few fresh chamomile flowers are a fragrant addition to salad. I enjoy a relaxing tea blend of fresh or dried chamomile, lavender, and lemon balm.

Harvesting chamomile

Harvest the flower heads at the peak of bloom to either use fresh or to dry for use in tea. In my experience, cutting the German chamomile down to one inch of foliage when it is fully blooming will spur a second growth of flowers.

CHERVIL

Anthriscus cerefolium

Culture

Chervil is an underappreciated culinary herb. Perhaps you recognize it as one of the herbs in the traditional French mixture *fines herbes*. Chervil is a cool season favorite of mine for planting in the spring and again in autumn. This low growing delicate plant with tiny leaves is very welcome in the spring, before other herbs are growing. Due to its diminutive stature, chervil is well suited to container gardening.

Planting chervil

An annual herb that prefers cooler weather, I plant chervil from seed in the spring. You can also purchase plant starters. If you plant from seed, keep in mind, chervil seeds need sunlight to germinate. Chervil will appreciate a partial sun location, either dappled sun throughout the day or morning sun only. It is not tolerant of hot weather or full bright sun. Chervil can be sown in 2-week successions like dill, radish, carrots, and lettuce for a harvest throughout spring.

Harvesting chervil

Harvest chervil as needed and use immediately. I enjoy the fresh leaves with the flavors of the spring garden: enjoy with baby beets, baby carrots, baby turnips, spinach, greens, and in egg dishes. A few chervil leaves in a spring greens and edible flower salad is delightful.

CHIVES

Garden or Onion Chives *Allium schoenoprasum*
Garlic or Chinese Chives *Allium tuberosum*

Culture

Chives are an herbaceous perennial herb that are one of the first to burst from the soil in spring. They grow well in Portland and are suited to in-ground, raised bed, or container gardening. Garden or onion chives are the most common and well-known type of culinary chives. Their tubular, grass-like leaves grow about 12 inches tall, with mild onion flavor, and bright round lavender-pink flowers. Those flowers are edible and are best harvested when they are young, before they turn papery. The flowers of this type of chives bloom in late spring.

Garlic or Chinese chives have flat, grass-like leaves growing about 20 inches tall, with spicier onion/garlic flavor and small, star-shaped white flowers held on umbrella-shaped clusters. The flowers of this type of chives bloom in mid- to late summer.

Planting chives

Chives are typically very winter hardy in Portland. Requiring only 6 hours of sunlight a day, chives can grow well in a less-sunny area of your garden. Plant both types of chives in the spring from seeds or starts.

Caring for chives

To keep them in check, trim chive flowers before they go to seed. After both types of chives flower, you can trim the entire plant down to the ground and it will grow back fresh leaves this season to extend your harvest. Since chives are a perennial herb, they will eventually develop into large clumps. During early spring or late fall, you can dig up entire plants and divide them every 3 years.

Harvesting chives

Harvest both types of chives by snipping the quantity you desire down to 1 inch of leaves. Chives can reseed themselves around your garden, especially the garlic type. Excess chive leaves freeze well for winter use.

CILANTRO

Coriandrum sativum

Culture

Cilantro is an annual herb that prefers the cooler weather of spring and fall. In fact, it is quite hardy here, sometimes lasting throughout a snowy winter. Cilantro tends to bolt in the hotter weather of summer.

Planting cilantro

Gardening students frequently tell me they have no luck growing cilantro. I think the key to success with cilantro is to plant it in the spring, skip the summer, and replant again in the fall. Since cilantro can be finicky with temperature fluctuations and prematurely bolt, I also recommend a monthly planting of cilantro in March, April, May and June. Cilantro can be planted from either seed or starts.

Cilantro care

Once cilantro bolts, the plant produces flowers and seeds and stops producing leaves. Cilantro's tiny white flowers are highly attractive to beneficial bugs, and the seeds are known as the spice coriander.

Harvesting cilantro

I prefer to use cilantro fresh, or, if there is an excess, by freezing. Cilantro loses its potent flavor with drying, so I do not recommend this preservation method. When my cilantro plant begins to bolt, I just leave it in the garden for its entire life cycle and then harvest the coriander seeds.

DILL

Anethum graveolens

Culture

If you have taken any of my classes, you have heard me refer to dill as our garden "ladybug daycare." In my experience, mature ladybugs lay their eggs on dill plants, and soon the plants are covered in tiny armored ladybug larvae, ferocious predators of aphids.

Dill is one of my number one companion plants in the edible garden. It is a frequent addition to cooking, it attracts beneficial bugs, it has ornamental value, and it can be included in floral arrangements.

Planting dill

Dill is a hardier warm season annual herb that can be planted in spring, around April, from both seeds and starts. I successively plant dill once a month in April, May, and June to ensure an uninterrupted harvest throughout the summer.

Depending on the variety, dill can grow up to 4 feet tall. For this reason, I usually give it a place towards the back/north side of the garden with other tall growing companion flowers like cosmos, Mexican sunflower, and zinnias. The pollen-laden yellow flowers of dill are magnets for bees and other beneficial bugs. The ferny foliage and lovely tiny yellow flowers make an excellent foliage addition to summery bouquets.

Dill care

Once dill plants have produced seed, they quickly end their life cycle and turn a yellowish-brown color. At this point, I pull out the dill plants completely, harvest the seed heads, and add the remaining dried plant to the compost bin. You can scatter the seeds around your garden for dill to sow again next year.

Harvesting dill

The ferny dill leaves can be harvested fresh or frozen for preservation. They are especially tasty directly added to salad greens, mixed in salad dressing, or sprinkled over potatoes, carrots, and beets.

Dill seeds are famous for their use in pickles. Harvest the whole flower heads with seeds for use in pickle recipes, or harvest and dry seeds for use in pickling spice blends, for baking in bread, or for seasoning recipes.

LAVENDER

Lavandula angustifolia or *L. officinalis* - English lavender
L. dentata - French lavender
L. x intermedia - Lavandin, Hedge lavender
L. stoechas - Spanish lavender

Culture

Lavender is a lovely ornamental plant in the garden, and its flowers are famous worldwide for their relaxing floral fragrance. An avid explorer into edible flowers, I frequently use the strong-tasting lavender flower in tea, salad dressing, and baking. Lavender buds are one of the ingredients in the *herbs de Provence* herb blend I adore using in carrot soup as well as with roast root vegetables, pork chops, and many chicken dishes.

Spring and summer blooming lavender flowers attract loads of bees to the garden, and their silvery evergreen foliage provides year-round interest.

There are many species and varieties of lavender. Depending on the variety, lavender can grow anywhere from 1 to 3 feet tall and wide. I grow several species and varieties of lavender in my garden.

Jolie's favorite varieties

Some of my favorite varieties for culinary use of their fragrant seeds are *Lavandula angustifolia*, Hidcote Blue, Munstead, and *L x intermedia* Grosso and Provence.

Planting lavender

Lavender is hardy to USDA zone 5 and is therefore reliably cold hardy in Portland (zone 8). Lavender is incredibly drought tolerant and well suited to xeriscaping and planting in the dreaded parking strip.

Lavender is an evergreen woody shrub. It can be planted throughout the year, though I recommend spring and fall planting. While it is a hardy small shrub, lavender does require full sun and excellent drainage. In poor drainage, lavender plants can succumb to root rot. Soil does not need to be rich, and the plants do not require supplement fertilization.

Lavender care

Lavender is drought tolerant and tolerates some neglect; however, to maintain a healthy-looking form, lavender should be pruned once a year every year. Lavender can be pruned in autumn by cutting back one third of the entire plant.

Harvesting lavender

Harvest lavender flowers just as they are blooming for fresh use and drying. Lavender flowers have a very strong, perfumy, floral fragrance and are best used in very small quantities in your culinary creations.

LEMON BALM

Melissa officinalis

Culture

Lemon balm sports deeply veined bright green leaves that are delightfully lemony-scented. Fresh lemon balm leaves, with their rich citrus flavor and scent, are delicious steeped for tea or added to salad dressings, fruit salad, and cold drinks. The leaves may be dried for a more potent tea. Lemon balm leaves can be frozen and dried for winter use.

Planting lemon balm

As a member of the mint family, lemon balm aggressively spreads by underground runners and self-sowing seeds. It can quickly become an invasive pest, taking over gardens. I always recommend planting lemon balm and all varieties of mint in containers to keep them contained.

An herbaceous perennial herb, lemon balm plants grow about 2 feet tall and wide. However, given space to run, in time they will spread as wide as your entire yard and into your neighbor's. I am not exaggerating. Like I said, keep them in check by always planting them in containers.

Lemon balm is super easy to grow. It requires full to partial sun and prefers moist soil. Plant by starts in the spring or fall. Ask a fellow gardener for a division to plant in your garden, and I'm sure they will be happy to share!

Lemon balm care

Lemon balm will perform best if the entire plant is pruned heavily two to three times during the growing season. Since I grow lemon balm in containers, I find the plants are the most vigorous if in the early spring I remove them from their pots, cut the root mass in half, and transplant each half in fresh potting soil. This way the plants don't become root bound and unproductive.

Harvesting lemon balm

Lemon balm can be harvested as needed for leaves to use fresh, dry, or freeze.

LEMON VERBENA

Aloysia triphylla

Culture

Lemon verbena's oily, slightly fuzzy, narrow green leaves are bursting with lemony fragrance and flavor. Their clusters of delicate white flowers are a delightful addition to the herb garden.

Planting lemon verbena

I recommend planting lemon verbena from a start in April-June. It prefers full sun, warm temperatures, and rich soil.

Lemon verbena care

Lemon verbena is a woody deciduous small shrub that grows to about 6 feet wide and tall and is hardy to about 10 degrees. However, this applies in the ideal growing conditions of its native South America. Here in Portland, I consider lemon verbena a borderline hardy/tender perennial herb.

I have yet to have a lemon verbena plant overwinter in my Portland garden, so I usually buy a new start every spring and grow it as a warm season annual herb. Lemon verbena can successfully overwinter in a greenhouse or sunny windowsill.

Harvesting lemon verbena

Harvest the leaves as needed throughout the season for fresh use steeped in tea, infusing water, in cold beverages, with fruit and fruit salad, and blended into smoothies or sorbet. For winter use, lemon verbena leaves can be dried or frozen.

LOVAGE

Levisticum officinale

Culture

Lovage is a pretty, ornamental plant with divided, glossy bright green leaves. It hails from the eastern Mediterranean and is an herbaceous perennial herb hardy down to zone 3. Lovage has a strong celery-like flavor and is grown for its leaves, seeds, and hallow stems. It is reliably hardy in Portland and a favorite in my summer herb garden.

The celery-flavored leaves, stems, and seeds of lovage make it a versatile herb in my kitchen. I use lovage leaves in salad dressing, to infuse vinegar, to flavor butter, added to green salads, in soup, and with peas, potatoes, and carrots.

Planting lovage

In the spring, plant lovage from starts. Alternatively, in the fall, you can direct seed lovage in the garden. In Portland, lovage prefers a full sun location with good drainage and regular watering.

Lovage care

Given ideal conditions, lovage can grow very large—up to 6 feet tall—so give it some space. In my experience, however, it has grown to be around 3 feet tall and wide. Established lovage plants can be dug and divided every couple of years.

Lovage can readily self-sow itself in the garden. To prevent this, prune off the seed heads as they develop.

Harvesting lovage

Harvest leaves as needed for fresh use in recipes. Leaves are tastiest when they are young, when the plant is less than 1 foot tall. During summer, hollow stems grow from the foliage clump and develop sprays of flat-topped greenish-yellow flower clusters. Flower clusters produce seeds. You can harvest seeds and dry them for recipes.

MARJORAM and OREGANO

Origanum spp.

Culture

Aromatic Italian oregano, Greek oregano, and marjoram are well known for sauces like pizza and marinara. I think oregano is delicious both fresh and dried in soup, stew, sauces, salads, meat dishes, and for infusing vinegar.

In my Portland garden, I grow Greek and Italian oregano varieties and their close relative, Sweet Marjoram. Oregano and marjoram have a pungent aroma from the essential oil carvacrol and are essential culinary herbs in my garden.

Planting marjoram and oregano

Greek and Italian type oreganos are hardy to zone 5 and grown as herbaceous perennial herbs in the Portland garden. Sweet marjoram is tender and is grown as an annual herb in Portland.

Plant both in spring by starts, cuttings, or divisions. Oregano and marjoram are well suited to in-ground, raised bed, and container gardens.

Marjoram and oregano care

Both oregano and marjoram require a full sun location in well-draining soil with little to no fertilizer. Plants require moderate watering and will rot in wet soil.

Be aware that stems can flop over and root into the soil, becoming a dense mat. If it becomes a nuisance, this can be prevented by regular harvesting. The small white flowers are very attractive to bees, beneficial bugs, and butterflies. However, once the plant is allowed to flower, it will produce fewer leaves. Pinch off the beginning of flower buds.

Typically, in Portland, the winter will kill off oregano foliage to the ground. If any woody stems remain over the winter, these older stems will also have much less leaf production. Prune the previous year's stems to the ground in winter or early spring.

Harvesting marjoram and oregano

Plants mature at 1 to 2 feet tall and wide. Frequently harvest the leaves for fresh use and drying.

MINT

Mentha spp.

Culture

Mint, with its crisp clean taste, will always have a home in my garden. I grow a half-dozen varieties of mint in my Portland garden, all in containers.

The most commonly grown and used mints are peppermint and spearmint, but there are many other varieties of mint! Fresh mint leaves are delicious with fruit and fruit salad, in sorbet and ice cream, in baking, in jellies and jams, and, of course, in hot tea and cold beverages. Mint leaves make a surprising and cooling addition to green salad, to Middle Eastern tabbouleh, to gazpacho, and when sprinkled over cucumber or carrots.

Jolie's favorite varieties

Some of my favorites are apple, chocolate, grapefruit, orange, and pineapple mints. Fresh chocolate mint leaves make the most refreshing summer iced tea or infused water.

Planting mint

Mint is an aggressive spreader, sending out underground runners in a tenacious quest to dominate your entire yard. Always grow mint in containers. Plant mint from starts or rooted cuttings in the spring or fall.

Mint care

Mint is an herbaceous perennial hardy to zone 5. It is reliably hardy in Portland and grows to about 2 feet tall and wide. Mint is a tough plant and requires little care. It can be grown in shadier spots but performs best in full sun, developing more fragrant and abundant leaves. Plants prefer moderate water and moist soil. In midsummer, plants bloom and attract loads of bees. However, to continue good leaf production and prevent reseeding, keep the flower head pruned off. Shear plants to the ground 2 to 3 times during the growing season for best shape and harvest. As I recommend always growing it in containers, each spring you should remove mint from its pot, divide the root mass in half, and replant in fresh potting soil.

Harvesting mint

Harvest mint leaves as needed for fresh and dried use.

PARSLEY

Petroselinum crispum

Culture

Parsley has gotten a bad rap, generally relegated to sprigs of the curly variety thrown on plates of diner food with an orange slice as a garnish. Its fresh taste is a must in my kitchen, and I love cooking with fresh parsley, from salad dressing to meatballs to steamed vegetables. Bright green, fresh parsley looks, smells, and tastes earthy and healthy. I aim to eat a serving of green leafy vegetables with every meal, and parsley is an excellent addition.

There are two types of parsley. Italian, or flat leaf, parsley is the common type for cooking. Curly parsley is typically used as a garnish and makes a pretty border plant in the ornamental garden.

Planting parsley

Plant parsley from starts in the spring or fall. Parsley does not grow very large, usually only about 12 inches tall and wide. It is well suited for container, raised bed, or in-ground gardens. I usually plant 3 parsley plants in the spring and replace them with 3 more in the early fall for an ample year-round harvest.

Parsley care

Parsley is a biennial herb, usually grown as an annual plant, and it is winter-hardy in Portland. This is exciting, since most of the herb garden has died down for the winter. Along with rosemary and cilantro, I can count on harvesting parsley throughout the winter in my Portland garden.

Both types of parsley require a full sun location with well-draining soil.

Harvesting parsley

Harvest parsley fresh from the garden as needed. Like most herbs, I typically add chopped fresh parsley to recipes when they are almost or completely cooked. Parsley can be preserved by the freezing method. I do not recommend drying parsley, as it loses so much of its flavor and fragrance. Besides, parsley is harvestable from your garden year-round in the Portland area.

ROSEMARY

Rosmarinus officinalis

Culture

Rosemary is an evergreen woody shrub, which can become quite large depending on the variety. Small blue flowers dot the stems in fall, winter, and into spring. In my Portland garden, I am delighted to see my rosemary plants bloom throughout the winter! Rosemary is a striking plant in the ornamental landscape, providing year-round interest with evergreen leaves, interesting branch structure, flowers, fragrance, and culinary use.

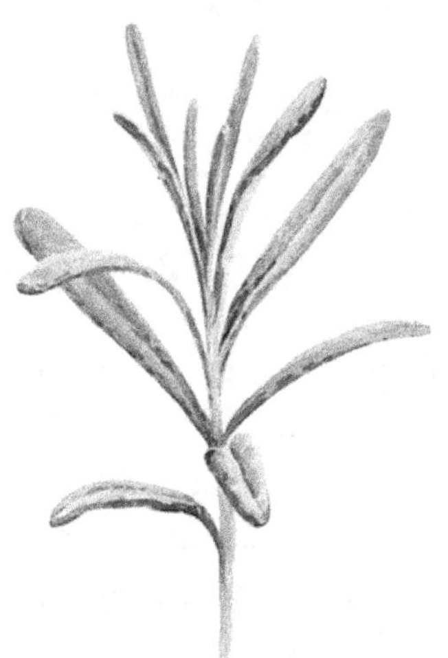

Planting rosemary

Rosemary is hardy to zone 8, which in Portland means that if we dip below our average zone 8 cold temperatures, a rosemary plant could die during the winter. Most rosemary plants are hardy in Portland, however, and can be seen as large shrubs in neighborhood yards.

Planting rosemary

Rosemary requires a full sun location with excellent draining soil. Plant rosemary in the spring or fall from starts. This pungent herb comes in both upright and trailing varieties. Both types of rosemary are suited to growing in containers.

Rosemary care

I often grow rosemary in a container for a few years and then transplant to an in-ground garden location. As the plants mature, make sure they have plenty of space.

Harvesting rosemary

Rosemary sports small, resinous, pine-needle shaped leaves. Harvest entire stems and strip the leaves by running your fingers down the stem. Finely mince strong flavored rosemary leaves and use sparingly.

You can also use entire stems to flavor roast vegetables and meat, soups, stews, and cold beverages. Straight, firm stems can be used whole as skewers for barbecuing meat and vegetables. Rosemary stems can be used to infuse vinegar. I think dried rosemary loses its potent flavor and fragrance. Since the plants are evergreen and harvestable throughout winter, I do not preserve any by drying or freezing.

SAGE

Salvia officinalis

Culture

Salvia is a large plant genus with over 900 species from around the world. Aromatic salvia includes culinary sage, as well as ornamental perennial and annual species.

Jolie's Favorite Varieties

My favorite culinary sage is Berggarten, with fuzzy green-gray wide oblong leaves. This cultivar is compact and bears large, rounded leaves, perfect for cooking. I also like to combine in a lovely container these three delightful colorful varieties: Icertina (gray-green leaves with yellow border), Purpurascens (red violet leaves when new fade to gray-green), and Tricolor (gray-green leaves with purplish pink and a cream border).

Planting sage

Hardy to zone 5, culinary sage is sometimes called common or garden sage. Sage is an herbaceous perennial that is reliably hardy in Portland, though sometimes it is subject to rotting in heavy clay during wet winters and springs. Plant sage from starts in spring or fall. Sage requires a full sun location with excellent drainage. There are numerous cultivars that range in size from 1 to 3 feet tall, usually growing wider than they are tall. Sage is well suited to container, raised bed or in-ground gardens.

Sage care

In my Portland garden, I have seen sage succumb to powdery mildew. When this happened, I have sheared the plant to the soil level, sprayed the nub with compost tea, and saturated the soil around it. When the plant grows back, the fungal disease is usually gone. Remember, you can prevent the spread of powdery mildew by watering with a wand, drip irrigation, or soaker hose instead of overhead watering.

Harvesting sage

Harvest whole sage leaves or stems as needed for fresh use. If your culinary sage is a cultivar that flowers, these are also edible. Sage is well known for its flavor in stuffing and poultry dishes. I can usually harvest fresh sage from my garden up to the Thanksgiving holiday before the plant dies back for the winter. I finely mince fresh sage to add to chicken soup and bread. I place entire leaves in the crockpot to flavor meat and vegetables, then remove before serving. I do not typically dry sage for winter use. I will, however, freeze entire leaves. Use sage to infuse vinegar or butter.

When I have an excess of sage, and when the plant would benefit from scaling back, I cut several stems from the base of the plant and use them as foliage accents in floral arrangements. Their pungent, fuzzy, soft leaves provide interesting background for flowers.

SAVORY

Satureja hortensis - Summer Savory
Satureja montana - Winter Savory

Culture

Savory is sometimes called "the bean herb," and until a few years ago was unknown in my Portland garden. There are two types of savory: summer savory is an annual, and winter savory is a semi-evergreen perennial. Both types of savory grow to about 18 inches tall and wide, with delicate white-lavender flowers favored by beneficial bugs. Their compact form is well suited to container, raised bed, or in-ground gardening.

Add whole sprigs to soups, stews, bean dishes, and roast meat and veggies. I include several whole savory sprigs in the crockpot when I'm making split pea or white bean and ham soups. Use savory to infuse vinegar, in salad dressing, and in egg dishes.

Planting savory

Both types of savory need a full sun location with well-draining soil and regular moisture. Plant savory from starts in spring.

Savory care

Being a perennial, winter savory benefits from pruning by shearing the plant to the ground 1 to 2 times during the active growing season. This will keep its shape from becoming rangy and woody.

Harvesting savory

Harvest savory leaves and sprigs as needed for fresh use.

SWEET BAY

Laurus nobilis

Culture

Sweet bay is a woody perennial that can take shrub or small tree form in Portland. Bay leaves provide flavor to a dish and do not taste good to eat, so make sure you remove and discard from your recipes before you serve them.

Planting sweet bay

Plant sweet bay from a good-sized starter plant in a sunny location with well-drained soil. Bay is suited to container gardening.

Sweet bay care

Sweet bay is a tender perennial, meaning it is only hardy down to zone 8. Portland is zone 8, so in a bad winter with extended low temperatures, ice, and snow, sweet bay may not be hardy.

Harvesting sweet bay

Fragrant leaves can be harvested as needed and used fresh or dried. Leaves become sweeter when dried. Like most dried herbs, sweet bay provides the most flavor when added to your recipe towards the end of cooking.

TARRAGON

Artemisia dracunculus

Culture

Tarragon, sometimes called French or true tarragon, is a unique tasting herb from the *Artemisia* family, which also includes wormwood and mugwort. Do not confuse French tarragon (*Artemisia dracunculus*), which can only be propagated by planting starts, with Russian tarragon (*Artemisia dracunculoides*), which I have seen sold as seeds and reputedly has inferior taste. To confuse the tarragon situation even more, there is another plant called Mexican tarragon or Mexican mint marigold (*Tagetes lucida*). Mexican tarragon has a similar licorice/anise taste as French tarragon. Mexican tarragon, with its bright yellow flowers, makes a cheery addition to the ornamental garden and as a companion plant. I recently saw it interplanted en masse with fuchsia-colored miniature zinnias in a botanical garden, and it was beautiful.

Freshly chopped tarragon is a favorite of mine in carrot soup or with roasted carrots. Infuse vinegar and make salad dressing with tarragon. Tarragon is a flavorful accent to an autumn apple and fennel salad.

Planting tarragon

Be sure to look for French tarragon plants at your local nursery in the late spring and early summer. Tarragon is an herbaceous perennial, and in my experience, it's one of the last herbs to emerge from the cool, wet spring soil. Tarragon is winter-hardy as far as temperatures are concerned—however, it needs well-drained soil and can rot out during especially wet winters and springs.

Plant tarragon in a full sun to partial shade location with good drainage. In my Portland garden, tarragon has not thrived when shaded out by other herb plants. Tarragon's compact size makes it ideal for container, raised bed, or in-ground gardens.

Tarragon care

Give tarragon regular watering during the active growing season.

Harvesting tarragon

Harvest tarragon as needed for fresh use. A little of the licorice/anise flavor of tarragon goes a long way, so use it sparingly. Tarragon preserves well both by drying and freezing.

THYME

Thymus vulgaris

Culture

Garden thyme, French thyme, and English thyme usually refer to the same plant, *Thymus vulgaris,* the most commonly used culinary thyme. Thyme is a compact plant spreading to about 12 inches tall and wider. Its tiny fragrant leaves are indispensable and versatile in the kitchen. A perennial herb, thyme is hardy to zone 5. In my experience, it remains semi-evergreen through winter in my Portland garden.

Thyme sports tiny white-pink flowers that are very attractive to bees and beneficial bugs. I frequently use fresh thyme flowers sprinkled over green salads, fruit, poultry, and steamed vegetables.

Orange Balsam is a cultivar of common thyme with an orange flavor. My garden would not be the same without Lemon Thyme *T. x citriodorus*—look for the variegated variety. It is super pretty as an ornamental plant, the bees love the tiny flowers, and the lemony taste of leaves and flowers are a delightful addition to so many dishes.

Planting thyme

Thyme requires a full sun location with fast-draining soil. Plant thyme in the spring or fall from starts. Due to its size, thyme is well suited to container, raised bed, or in-ground gardens. I utilized thyme's spreading, trailing growth habit by planting it around the edge of raised beds and containers.

Thyme care

Perennial thyme can be long-lived and benefits from a pruning at least once a year in the spring by shearing foliage by one third. This will prevent long woody stems with few leaves and promote a lush growth habit and abundant harvest.

In my experience, lemon thyme often does not overwinter and needs to be replaced each spring.

Harvesting thyme

Thyme can be harvested as needed throughout the growing season for fresh use. Strip the stems of tiny leaves by gently rubbing your fingers down the stem. The work can seem tedious, but I assure you, the flavor of fresh thyme leaves are worth the extra work. Thyme dries well and also makes a delicious iced or hot tea.

Notes

Notes

Notes

Resources

Recommended Gardening Books

These are some favorite gardening books from my own library.

Bellamy, Andrea. 2010. *Sugar Snaps and Strawberries*. Portland, OR. Timber Press.

Bradley, Fern Marshall. 2007. *Rodale's Vegetable Garden Problem Solver*. Emmaus, PN. Rodale Press Inc.

Colebrook, Binda. 2013. *Winter Gardening in the Maritime Northwest: Cool Season Crops for the Year-Round Gardener-5th Edition*. Gabriola Island, BC, Canada. New Society Publishers.

Coleman, Eliot. 1993. *The New Organic Growers's Four Season Harvest*. White River Junction, VT. Chelsea Green Publishing.

Creasy, Rosalind. 2010. *Edible Landscaping*. San Francisco, CA. Sierra Club Books.

Cunningham, Sally Jean. 1998. *Great Garden Companions*. Emmaus, PN. Rodale Press Inc.

Forkner, Lorene Edwards. 2013. *The Timber Press Guide to Vegetable Gardening in the Pacific Northwest*. Portland, OR. Timber Press.

Jabbour, Nikki. 2011. *The Year-Round Vegetable Gardener*. North Adams, MA. Storey Publishing.

Pears, Pauline. 2002. *Rodale's Illustrated Encyclopedia of Organic Gardening*. New York, NY. DK Publishing.

Riotte, Louise. 1975. *Carrots Love Tomatoes*. North Adams, MA. Storey Publishing.

Solomon, Steve and Marina McShane. 2015. *Growing Vegetables West of the Cascades 35th Anniversary Edition.* Seattle, WA. Sasquatch Books.

Editors of *Sunset* books. *Sunset Western Garden Book of Edibles.* Oxmoor House, 2010.

Taylor, Lisa. 2014. *Maritime Northwest Garden Guide.* Seattle, WA. Seattle Tilth.

Local Nurseries and Garden Centers

I support locally owned and operated nurseries and garden centers. I encourage you to do the same. Here are some around the Portland metro area

Al's Garden Center
7505 SE Hogan Road
Gresham, OR 97080
Locations also in Sherwood,
    Wilsonville, and Woodburn
als-gardencenter.com

Birds and Bees Nursery
3327 SE 50th Ave
Portland, OR 97206
503-788-6088
birdsandbeespdx.com

Cornell Farms
8212 SW Barnes Rd
Portland OR 97225
cornellfarms.com

Dennis' 7 Dees
10455 SW Butner Road
Portland OR
1090 McVey Ave
Lake Oswego OR
dennis7dees.com

Drake's 7 Dees
5645 SW Scholls Ferry Rd
Portland OR 97225
drakes7dees.com

Farmington Gardens
21815 SW Farmington Rd
Beaverton OR 97007
466 SE Baseline
Hillsboro OR 97123
farmingtongardens.com

Garden Fever! Nursery
3433 NE 24th Ave
Portland OR 97212
gardenfever.com

Linnton Feed & Seed
10920 NW Saint Helens Rd
Portland OR 97231
linntonfeed.com

Marbott's Greenhouse & Nursery
1808 NE Columbia Blvd
Portland OR 97211
marbotts.com

One Green World
6469 SE 134th Ave
Portland OR 97236
onegreenworld.com

Pistils Nursery
3811 N. Mississippi Ave
Portland OR 97227
pistilsnursery.com

Portland Nursery
9000 SE Division
Portland OR 97266

5050 SE Stark
Portland OR 97215
portlandnursery.com

Shorty's Garden Center
10006 Mill Plain Blvd
Vancouver, WA 98664
shortysgardencenter.com

Tony's Garden Center
10300 SE Holgate Blvd
Portland OR 97266
tonysgarden.com

Yard N Garden Land
1501 NE 102nd Ave
Vancouver, WA 98686
yardngardenland.com

Afterword

IN JANUARY 2019, as my first editor and I were busily working on this book, my husband and I unexpectedly had to move from our rental home and beloved garden of eight years. Though we were given two months, it was a surprise and certainly a stress. My garden is the source of inspiration and the foundation of my garden writing and teaching. Not only is my garden a place of sanctuary and a producer of food but it is also my avocation, vocation, and livelihood.

We scrambled to quickly find another place to live before my busy spring work season began. Faced with digging and potting up my extensive garden during mid-winter posed a significant challenge, particularly locating the dormant herbaceous perennials. Within thirty minutes of sending an email to my gardening community requesting used plastic pots, my friends at Portland Nursery donated hundreds of them.

Grateful for the relatively mild weather and that my health was in a stable period, we were blessed with several dry days, and over the course of five days, Jay and I dug and potted up close to two hundred plants. Evergreen and deciduous shrubs, conifers, Japanese maples, natives, perennials, bulbs, herbs, fruit, ferns, ornamental grasses, and groundcovers prepared for their move across town. We dismantled trellises, packed up gardening tools, furniture, and décor. One cedar raised bed frame we built was emptied of soil and joined us on the move. What would come with us? What would go into storage? This endeavor was physically and emotionally taxing.

On a cold weekend in early February, our loving community of friends rallied together with their trucks, SUVs, and cars to transport our massive garden to our transitional home. Today, my best friend Catherine jokes with a smile, "Remember that one time we moved The Gardening Goddess?" This epic plant journey will go down in our community's history, and I am forever grateful to our large group of friends that did not hesitate or doubt when I said that I needed to dig and move my entire mature garden.

We anxiously loaded up our moving truck as snowflakes gently fell, followed by angry hail, strong downpours, and sunbreaks. With both great sorrow and hope for the future, we moved into our transitional home with a friend in Southeast Portland who welcomed our massive plant collection and us. Within one week of being at our new home, our potted plant collection was subjected to two snowfalls, temperatures in the twenties, and wind chill in the teens. Time will tell how our potted garden survives.

For 2019 and 2020, the plants remained in their pots, and with regular watering, we suffered only a few losses. Those springs and summers, I grew vegetables and herbs in the one raised bed we brought, along with a multitude of containers. It was the smallest vegetable garden I've had in almost a decade. Our transitional home in the Richmond neighborhood was a warmer microclimate than above the Alameda ridge in the Concordia neighborhood of our old home. While I grieved the loss of my old secret garden, the garden I poured my heart and soul into, I was up for my new gardening challenge.

As a renter, gardens come and go. Through the past twenty-plus years, I have built and grown eight different gardens, including two community gardens and three strictly container gardens at apartments. The garden I left was by far the most significant garden I had ever grown, and I will always remember it as my magical secret garden, a place of incredible tranquility and healing.

Nature is one of my greatest teachers. No matter how much work, energy, input, and expectation I have in my garden, nature always determines the outcome. I cannot control the weather, the climate, the plants, the pests, the disease or the wildlife. Gardening is certainly a wonderful metaphor for life. Nothing is ever really certain, even housing. My experience with moving is not unique. When we found out we had to move, I heard from numerous gardeners about similar experiences with their rentals and having to uproot their gardens.

In early 2020, all of our lives changed dramatically due to the COVID-19 pandemic. I shifted my work and teaching to remote. As an immune-compromised person living with multiple chronic illnesses, I strictly sheltered at home. Gardening virtual classes have continued to be extremely popular. We saw an epic increase in gardening due to the pandemic, and my hope is that all of these new gardeners will stay lifelong gardeners.

By summer 2020, Jay and I were finally ready to purchase our first home. The 2020 real estate market was incredibly competitive. We diligently searched four counties within a one-hour radius of Portland. After viewing dozens of homes and putting in multiple offers, we finally read a listing for a sweet 1968 ranch on .19 acres in Washington County: "nice mix of sun and shade, mature fruit trees, gardened organically for over thirty years." That description alone spoke volumes to us, and the moment we stepped inside, we knew we were home. Our offer was accepted within twenty-four hours of the home going on the market.

In September 2020, our loyal masked friends once again packed up our two hundred potted plants and transported them to our new home. Due to the pandemic, this was the first time I'd seen most of our friends in six months. Home ownership is an incredible adventure, and I have tremendous gratitude. Starting a new garden from scratch on the largest lot I've ever lived on is exciting and a lot of hard work.

Sharing this story with you now seems like a fitting way to end this book I am so passionate about. Through the years, I have greatly enjoyed sharing the photos and experience from my old garden with you in my writing and teaching. In the old home, I envisioned, proposed, wrote, and edited this book. In my transitional home, I documented my temporary gardening activities and created all of my gardening virtual classes. I think it is poignant that I am excitedly releasing this gardening book into the world from my new garden.

Thank you for coming along the ride with me in my various gardens. As this book launches, I want to thank you for your readership. I look forward to sharing with you my new gardening adventure as a first-time first-generation home owner.

Warmly,
Jolie Ann Donohue
The Gardening Goddess
Healing People, Communities, and the Earth One Garden at a Time

Index

About the Author

THE GARDENING GODDESS Jolie Ann Donohue is a garden designer, consultant, educator, and writer. An edible gardening expert, her popular organic gardening classes have drawn a diverse group of gardeners at a variety of venues including Portland Nursery, Portland Community College, Mt. Hood Community College, local garden clubs, and numerous non-profit organizations. As a therapeutic gardening specialist, she has spread the healing power of nature in hospitals, pediatrics, rehabilitation, skilled nursing, long term care, memory care, assisted living, and vocation training. She joyfully lives and gardens just outside of Portland, Oregon, and you can connect with her at jolieanndonohue.com. This is her first book.

www.ingramcontent.com/pod-product-compliance
Lightning Source LLC
Chambersburg PA
CBHW080442030726

47592CB00011B/2939